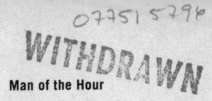
Man of the Hour

Foolishly, or at least naively, Abraham did not gather a team of experienced professionals before his astonishing news was made public. When he appeared at the television station to accept the big check that night, he had no lawyers or financial experts standing by in the greenroom to whisk away his newfound wealth to some fiduciary fortress, and no one to shield him from the swarm of supplicants who began begging from him within hours of the word getting out.

There are legends about jackpot winners being besieged by long-lost cousins and self-declared best friends, not to mention out-and-out scam artists with "can't-lose" propositions. Abraham must have heard them, too, but his had been such a simple and obscure existence that he might not have grasped that he was now a celebrity, and he certainly didn't know how to behave like one. Nothing in his experience would have prepared him for how aggressive people could be when a human treasure chest suddenly appears in their midst.

UNLUCKY NUMBER

The Murder of Lottery Winner
Abraham Shakespeare

DEBORAH MATHIS
with GREGORY TODD SMITH

BERKLEY BOOKS, NEW YORK

THE BERKLEY PUBLISHING GROUP
Published by the Penguin Group
Penguin Group (USA) LLC
375 Hudson Street, New York, New York 10014

USA • Canada • UK • Ireland • Australia • New Zealand • India • South Africa • China

penguin.com

A Penguin Random House Company

UNLUCKY NUMBER

A Berkley Book / published by arrangement with the author

For information, address: The Berkley Publishing Group,
a division of Penguin Group (USA) LLC,
375 Hudson Street, New York, New York 10014.

ISBN: 978-0-425-27491-0

PUBLISHING HISTORY
Berkley premium edition / February 2015

PRINTED IN THE UNITED STATES OF AMERICA

10 9 8 7 6 5 4 3 2 1

Cover design by Oysterpond Press.
Cover photos: *Money background* © Aleksander
Bryliaev / Shutterstock; *Feet* © Pamela Moore / Istock photo.

To Moses and Jeremiyah,
who we hope have inherited their father's good heart.

ACKNOWLEDGMENTS

Writing a book can be cathartic. It can be exhilarating. It can be rewarding. But it is always hard and time-consuming work. The writer has to lay many other activities and engagements—and people—aside during the research and writing process. So, patient, loving, and forgiving kin contribute as much to the final product as anyone, perhaps more, given that they provide the love, nourishment, and understanding that allow the writer to spend hours upon hours in solitary confinement, of little use to anyone or anything else.

For that reason, I must thank my loved ones for putting up with my absences, moodiness, and preoccupation over the course of this important book project. They understood that this story had to be told, and no matter how remiss I was when it came to their needs, they only talked about mine. I am, as always and forever, grateful for this marvelous bunch. I am also grateful to my sister and her husband for making the introductions that made this book happen. My daughter, Allison, provided priceless service and relief to me as my research assistant and helpmate.

Many thanks to my literary agent, Jill Marsal, who believed in this project from the start and saw it to fruition, notwithstanding her sometimes unwieldy client.

Gregory Todd Smith is the hero of this story, and he is my new, true friend. I am grateful for his honesty, availability, patience, and trust in me to tell his story. Many writers wanted to do it and could have. He chose me, and I am honored by that choice.

On Gregory's behalf, I would also like to thank Sergeants David Wallace, David Clark, and Christopher Lynn, of the Polk County Sheriff's Office. They entrusted Greg to help them break the case and not only promised to have his back, but had it. Their dedication and skill are a tribute to law enforcement. Greg also wishes to thank Polk County sheriff Grady Judd, who committed the manpower and resources it took to ensure that an illiterate, often homeless, but kindhearted man's murder did not go unnoticed and unpunished.

—DEBORAH MATHIS

PREFACE

In March 2014, on the brink of the annual college-basketball showdown known as March Madness, billionaire Warren Buffett teamed with Quicken Loans to concoct a get-rich-quick scheme to beat all. They would pay $1 billion to anyone, eighteen or older, who correctly predicted the winners of every game in the sixty-three-game national tournament. Even with the number of contestants limited (one per household) to fifteen million entries, the odds of winning were a mind-numbing one in nine quintillion. But that didn't stop people from trying. (Unsurprisingly, no one won Buffett's bracket contest. No one even came close. Most people were eliminated on day one; no one remained by the end of day two.)

Although Buffett's March Madness bracket scheme was not a lottery per se, like a lottery, it was a game of chance and showed, once again, that the dream of striking it suddenly and gloriously rich is alive and well. Not even absurd, nearly impossible odds can quell it.

Lotteries have been a part of the United States since its very founding, when tickets to games of chance were sold to help fund the development of some colonies (such as Jamestown, Virginia), and at one point were considered not only a viable way to raise revenue for public causes, but a civically responsible one. At one time, all thirteen original colonies had a lottery to raise revenue for public services. But, in time, the lotteries became riddled with bribery, payout defaults, and other corruption. They fell into such disrepute that evangelical reformers were able to successfully press a moral argument for prohibition, and by 1895, government-run lotteries were banned nationwide.

The lottery's official comeback took nearly three quarters of a century, beginning in New Hampshire in 1964. Today, armed with regulations and safeguards, forty-four states, plus the District of Columbia, Puerto Rico, and the U.S. Virgin Islands, all sponsor lotteries. Only Alabama, Alaska, Hawaii, Mississippi, Nevada, and Utah abstain.

Both religious and public policy advocates routinely oppose lotteries (the former usually due to biblical strictures, and the latter typically out of concern over the government's reliance on fantasy-fueled games of chance to fund essential services like public education), but state and multistate lotteries are wildly popular among the masses. It is estimated that about 120 million American men and women—half of all adults in the country—play state-run lotteries each year, accounting for $45 billion in receipts. Only about 1,600 of them will win a million dollars or more. The rest of us have to settle for a few bucks, if we're at all lucky, or more likely just add the useless slips to our pile of poor choices. The summer house in the Hamptons, the ski chalet in Saint Moritz, the foundation we were going to endow, the freedom from indebtedness, and the ability to tell the boss to take this job and shove it—all will have to live a bit longer in our fantasies and most likely will live there forever. But hope springs eternal that Fortune will make a rewarding pit stop our way. Indeed, the randomness of a lucky strike is part of the lottery's appeal. It can happen to anyone, from any walk of life, and in even the most obscure places.

In May 2013, Gloria McKenzie, an eighty-four-year-old widow originally from rural Maine, now living in Zephyrhills, Florida, was in line at a local supermarket to buy an auto-generated Powerball ticket when the kindly young woman in front of her stepped aside, allowing Mrs. McKenzie to go first. She thanked the woman for the courtesy, bought her $2 ticket and left. Chosen at random by a machine, the ticket Mrs. McKenzie walked away with that day contained the winning numbers in the multistate lottery. Her jackpot was almost $600 million—$590,500,000, the largest in the multistate game's twenty-one-year history and the second largest in the annals of American lotteries. By sheer luck, Mrs. McKenzie had beaten odds calculated at one in 175 million.

Like most big jackpot winners, Mrs. McKenzie elected the lump-sum option for her payday, about $371,000,000 before taxes. She sank back into obscurity after collecting her winnings in Tallahassee two months after the drawing, where she emerged accompanied by her son and two law-yers, and thus adhering to the first rule suggested by experts who study those lucky few who hit it big: get a team.

Financial planner Susan Bradley told the *Palm Beach Post* shortly after the big drawing that she provides the super-high-dollar clients she advises with a team of neuro-psychologists, estate-planning attorneys, and other profes-sionals to help them navigate the treacherous waters of over-the-top wealth. These teams are meant to help insu-late her clients from scam artists, bad investments, tricky temptations, and the deluge of hangers-on who typically prey upon the superrich. Bradley has a special set of do's and don'ts for the suddenly and sensationally wealthy.

"One of the first things to do is stop answering the phone," Bradley told the newspaper. "Get a cell phone with a new number and only give it to your inner circle people and keep that circle small."

Gloria McKenzie has apparently handled her wild for-tune smartly. She is said to still shop at big-box stores and frequent neighborhood eateries, though she once paid for the meals of a restaurant full of diners. Reportedly, she has built a multimillion-dollar home in Jacksonville, Florida, but has otherwise been frugal, still tooling around "in her son's old Ford Focus," according to one news account.

Mrs. McKenzie's is not the only good news story about lottery winners. There are many that end happily—or happily enough. Who doesn't rejoice at the news that a fat jackpot has been claimed by a downtrodden single mother who rides three buses to her menial job each day? Who isn't inspired by the Missouri couple who, after netting more than $136,000,000 from Powerball, poured loads of money into improving their town, including a new fire station, ball field, sewage-treatment plant, and a scholarship fund at their high school alma mater?

There's also the story of Sheelah Ryan, of Florida, who used her $55 million winnings in a 1988 lottery to endow a foundation that provided assistance for poor people, single mothers, children, the elderly, and homeless animals.

But, when things go wrong for lottery winners, they can go awfully wrong. News accounts, police files, and court records are full of instances where winning was far from the panacea that most people imagine when handing over a few dollars in hopes of collecting a king's ransom.

One of the most famous instances of good luck gone bad is that of Jack Whittaker, a West Virginian who won a $315,000,000 Powerball jackpot in 2002. The next seven years were riddled with misfortune. Whittaker was robbed several times, once to the tune of $545,000; on another occasion, he was taken for $200,000. In a three-month period, both his granddaughter and her boyfriend died of drug overdoses. And Caesar's Palace, the legendary Las Vegas casino, sued him for $1.5 million worth of bad checks he had written to cover his gambling losses. At one point, Whittaker lamented that he hadn't destroyed his winning ticket.

And there's William Post, of Pennsylvania, a $16 million lottery winner. His landlady conned him out of a small fortune, his brother tried to hire a hit man to kill him, and he ended up smothered in debt.

And there's Janite Lee, who, choosing the annual payout instead of lump sum, was collecting $620,000 a year but ended up in such straits that she sold her rights to the annual payments and still went bankrupt.

Some sad endings are worse than others. Like many other winners, the man at the center of this story neglected to surround himself with wise, experienced counsel but rather relied on old friends and his own well-meaning but often misguided instincts to help him manage his multi-million-dollar winnings. It was a haphazard way to proceed and did nothing to ward off the constant appeals for money from all corners—a pestilence that turned the normally easygoing man into a miserable wreck.

When a stranger came along nearly a year after he won the lottery, not asking for money but offering help, he was eager to take it. She told him about the successful business she ran, about the money she made, and convinced him that she could assist him in getting his finances under control. Uneducated, weary, and in over his head, he accepted her offer and turned over control of his funds and outstanding accounts to her. Then he vanished.

This is the story of the peculiar, egregious connivances of a woman who might have gotten away with her crimes had she not met a man who was more cunning than she.

It is a tale of double betrayal of trust, of a man who meant well, and of a woman overcome by greed and delusion. It is the sad truth of what happened to a man who beat the long odds of winning a state lottery only to lose his most prized possession—his life.

CHAPTER ONE

#####

What's in a Name?

—*ROMEO AND JULIET*, BY WILLIAM SHAKESPEARE

If ever there was a name built for distinction, it was Abraham Lee Shakespeare. A name that brings to mind patriarchs and liberators and literary geniuses. Yet most of forty-three-year-old Abraham Shakespeare's life had been a patchwork of hustles, a steady stream of challenges to make it from one sunrise to the next, forever on the run from deprivation, danger, or incarceration.

Born in the small central Florida town of Sebring as the youngest of Elizabeth Walker's four children, Abraham had come up even rougher than others in his low-income, racially estranged environment; he dropped out of school after the seventh grade and went to join his father, James, working in the citrus groves that help fuel the Florida economy and account for its standing as one of the world's top citrus producers. It was questionable how much schooling he'd absorbed anyway, given that he could barely read and write. What education he did have had failed him, leaving him a loiterer on the outskirts of mainstream society, unskilled and unsettled. When he was thirteen, a conviction for theft got Abraham sent away to what people used to call "reform school"—a state-run juvenile detention facility—and he remained there until he was eighteen.

In the hardscrabble black neighborhoods of Lakeland, no one seemed to have any qualms about the tall, lanky man with the dreadlocked hair who pretty much kept to himself, laid low, and lived with his father. When James Shakespeare died of heart disease in 2005 at age eighty-four, Abraham moved in with his mother, Elizabeth Walker, sharing her tiny house on East Lowell Street in Lakeland's rough-and-tumble Lakeside Addition.

Although Lakeland is a much larger city with more to do than in Sebring, where he grew up, the move did little to improve Abraham's lot. He was still unable to find or make a place for himself in the mainstream and become productive and self-supporting. Hanging out—and hanging on—was his daily recourse, and Abraham was no stranger to small clubs and bars where people without much means or much else to do would gather to dance, drink, and laugh their troubles away.

Always fond of the ladies, he had romanced Antoinette Andrews, a woman he had known since childhood, and with her had produced a son in 1998. They named the child Moses.

By all accounts, Abraham adored his boy. Even though his relationship with Antoinette was off and on, Abraham was an attentive father. According to Antoinette, Abraham never let more than a week pass without at least a phone call to Moses, and he would usually see his son three to four times a week. Unfortunately, Abraham's pocketbook could not match his heart. He was almost always a day late and a dollar short in what he owed Antoinette for their son's care, and he was forever dodging child-support enforcement officials. A few times, he was even locked up for failing to make his court-ordered payments.

For the most part, Abraham owed his survival and freedom to near misses and dumb luck. By his fourth decade of life, he was still an unaccomplished and pitiable figure whose youth had been pestered by discrimination, poverty, and mischief and whose only noteworthy adult exploits were confined to several pages of police reports and prison records.

If he hadn't scored a day-labor job washing dishes or loading trucks, Abraham could usually be found hanging around Lakeland's Super Choice Foods, a convenience store, talking about next to nothing with similarly idle friends, all the while admiring and flirting with the women who passed through the area. Super Choice was owned by a burly fellow of Arab descent named Jimard Yuseff Zaid, whom everyone called Papi. Papi took a liking to Abraham and used him to run errands for him and his business. It was Papi's name on the cell phone in Abraham's pocket, and the few dollars that Abraham might have at any given moment were as likely to have come from Papi as from anyone.

Most who bothered to know him found the quiet,

easygoing Abraham Shakespeare unremarkable but likable and harmless. No one really considered Abraham a menace or a threat. After all, he never hurt anyone. Some even came to consider him a friend. One of those people was local barbershop owner Gregory Todd Smith. The two first met in 1999, when Abraham strolled into Greg's barbershop on Fifth Street one day and asked if there were any odd jobs he could do to earn a few bucks.

At first, Greg was tempted to give this unexpected visitor the boot. After all, if he had to get up every day and pull a regular nine to five, why shouldn't this able-bodied fella? Besides, Greg thought, people like Abraham were bad for business.

But just as Greg was about to kick the man out, an old memory surfaced and short-circuited that plan. He recalled how his grandfather, long gone now, had more than once led a neighborhood wino to some spot where a chore needed doing, later coming out of his pocket with a few dollars for the transient. Granddaddy had always said a little change for some honest work would keep folks from stealing and robbing people, and Granddaddy was always right. Almost absentmindedly, Greg found himself taking Abraham around the barbershop, pointing out what needed to be cleaned, straightened, moved, or thrown out in exchange for cash on the spot.

It was the start of what would become a familiar routine. Two or three days a week, Abraham would show up and set to work at Greg's place, then either leave with a few bills in his pocket or hang out to shoot the shit in the barbershop, which—like neighborhood barbershops everywhere—served as a sounding board and listening post for men eager to unwind and talk candidly about women, sports, politics, money, and the latest community scuttlebutt. Abraham developed easy friendships with Greg and many of his regulars, who appreciated the taciturn wanderer for his easygoing spirit, wry sense of humor, street sense, and kind heart.

Notwithstanding Abraham's many deficiencies—no education, no home of his own, no particular talent or skills, no reliable source of income, and seemingly no plans for the future—Greg considered Abraham to be a gifted man for his temperament and good nature alone. Before long, he was calling his new friend by the nickname he had coined just for him: Shakyboy, a play on Abraham's surname.

Several months after Shakyboy had appeared out of nowhere and become part of the landscape on Greg's block, he disappeared. Two or three weeks went by with no sign or sighting of the man, and no one seemed to know why. Though he couldn't help but notice Abraham's absence, Greg did not worry, assuming that soon enough Shakyboy would show up again and resume his old routines.

Then one day, as Greg stood outside the shop to have a cigarette, he spotted Abraham in an orange uniform on the back of a City of Lakeland garbage truck as it passed down Fifth Street. A sanitation job may not be what most people aspire to, but it meant steady work and reliable paydays, and Greg felt a surge of pride when he saw his friend on that truck that day.

As was unfortunately typical, however, Abraham didn't keep that job for long and soon was back to looking for day work. But even after he gained and lost several other jobs, Abraham kept up his habit of dropping by Greg's barbershop, even when Greg moved his business to other locations. Abraham often had something going on, jobwise—dishwashing, hauling and loading, one- or two-day gigs on construction sites, that kind of thing. It was a hell of a way to stitch together a living, but he seemed to make it work, and as long as grit and brawn were in demand somewhere, Greg was convinced his friend Shakyboy would be all right. Besides, he had more to do than worry about some other fully grown man.

Business was booming at Greg's new barbershop location on Highway 98 North, the most travelled stretch of roadway in Lakeland. Greg's client base had quickly grown, and the place became a hot spot for the *Madden NFL* video-game tournaments he hosted, drawing both small- and big-time gamers alike to hang out all day, playing for money and running their mouths. If anything of any interest was going on around town, one of the regulars at Greg's barbershop was bound to know about it, and make sure everyone else did, too.

On Thursday, November 16, 2006, all the shop crowd could talk about was the lucky so-and-so who had hit the $31 million Florida lottery the night before. Even though most of the customers in the shop had played the lottery that week too, no one expressed any real envy or dejection over not having won, considering the absurdly long odds of winning a jackpot big enough to forever and dra-

matically change their lives. No one even bothered to speculate who the winner actually was; instead, the men carried
on for hours describing how they would've spent money
like that, all of them one-upping the other with the quality
or quantity of the things they would buy or do with a bank
account beyond their imaginations, their fantastical talk
conjuring up mansions, yachts, Ferraris, and business ven-
tures galore.

By the next day, however, word spread that, unbeliev-
ably, the 31-million-dollar winner was someone they
all knew—none other than that alien to good fortune,
Abraham Shakespeare.

Greg found the claim outlandish. "Someone just trying to start some shit," he said to the assembled crowd
in his shop, raising the clippers to a client's temple.
"Shakyboy ain't got two nickels to rub together, let
alone buy a lottery ticket." A chorus of "Amen" swelled
in the shop.

But Greg was wrong about his friend. It turned out
that Abraham *had* purchased a lottery ticket on that fateful Wednesday, November 15—not only one, but two.
Abraham and Michael Ford, both then working as deliv-
erymen for a Lakeland food-distribution company named
the MBM Corporation, had set out early that day to
deliver a truckload of meat to restaurants in Miami, with
Ford at the wheel. As the men pulled into the Town Star
convenience store in Frostproof, Ford hopped out to buy
some sodas and cigarettes. "Get me two quick picks!"
Abraham shouted as Ford walked toward the store. Ford
returned with two tickets, each bearing a row of six

computer-generated numbers, and Abraham handed Ford two of the five dollars he had to his name.

When the drawing occurred later that night, Abraham was astonished to learn that one of his two sets of numbers was the winning combination: 6, 12, 13, 34, 42, and 52. Soon after, he shared the good news with a few family members and friends, including Greg. A couple of days later, he was on TV in Tallahassee, wearing a Florida Lottery T-shirt, with his long dreadlocks tucked inside a Rastafarian bonnet and his mother and two sisters helping him hold up a sign made up to look like an oversize check that read "Abraham Lee Shakespeare. $31 Million! Lotto Jackpot."

News accounts across the Sunshine State reported that the latest lucky winner had done as most big lottery winners do and had elected to take an immediate payout of a lesser lump sum rather than receive the $31 million in annual increments over twenty years. That lump sum came to just under $17 million before taxes—about $12 million after the IRS had its way—meaning the illiterate day laborer who used to sweep freshly cut hair off Greg Smith's floors, drink a little too much hooch at times, and handle other people's garbage was suddenly worth a mint. When a television news reporter asked Abraham what it meant to be an overnight multimillionaire, he replied, with conspicuous relief, "I don't have to struggle no more."

CHAPTER TWO

......

Abraham Shakespeare's enormous good luck with the state lottery certainly took care of his day-to-day struggles, but he was not trouble-free. Almost immediately, he discovered that old hassles and challenges had been replaced by new and, in some ways, bigger ones.

Foolishly, or at least naively, Abraham did not gather a team of experienced professionals before his astonishing news was made public. When he appeared at the television station to accept the big check that night, he had no lawyers or financial experts standing by in the greenroom to whisk away his newfound wealth to some fiduciary fortress, and no one to shield him from the swarm of supplicants who began begging from him within hours of the word getting out.

A mere week after Abraham's big win, the State of Florida came after him for more than $9,000 in court costs and back child support owed to Antoinette Andrews. The state not only collected the nine grand, but also saw to it that Abraham set up a million-dollar trust for his son. Despite the embarrassingly public way Abraham came to make good on his obligation to Moses, no one who knew Abraham believed he had any problem with turning the money over for his son's care. The restitution had been thrust upon him suddenly, but Abraham didn't seem to have a problem with it.

Before long, Abraham would have another child to care for. His former live-in girlfriend, Sentorria Butler, gave birth to a boy named Jeremiah in November 2008. Abraham and Sentorria—whom everyone called Torrie—had broken up not long before Jeremiah was born, and although Abraham was apparently a doting father to begin with, the two parents often butted heads over Abraham's alleged derelictions in providing for the baby. Eventually, their relationship became contentious enough to involve the courts and a war of words.

Rumor had it that Abraham offered to buy a new house for his mother, who had worked for many years in school cafeterias, but that Elizabeth Walker turned down the offer, worried that she wouldn't be able to afford the property taxes and insurance on a new home. Whatever amount her quaint concern may have saved her son, however, was in short order consumed by the gift and loan seekers who continued to stream past Abraham's door with sob stories and elaborate schemes in tow.

There are legends about jackpot winners being besieged

by long-lost cousins and self-declared best friends, not to mention out-and-out scam artists with "can't-lose" propositions. Abraham must have heard them too, but his had been such a simple and obscure existence that he might not have grasped that he was now a celebrity, and he certainly didn't know how to behave like one. Nothing in his experience would have prepared him for how aggressive people could be when a human treasure chest suddenly appears in their midst.

People descended upon Shakyboy from everywhere. And out of nowhere. Somebody had a loved one to bury but no insurance or money for a funeral; Abraham gave them the money. He did that four or five times, sometimes handing thousands of dollars over to people he'd never even met until they came pleading for help. He gave loads of money to his friends and, on at least one occasion, to the adult children of a friend because the elder man had been good to Abraham through the years. He loaned Papi $1 million. He cured people's tax, rent, and utility-bill delinquencies. He paid off other people's mortgages, medical bills, and car loans. The textbook and tuition bills of one or two college students were satisfied, courtesy of Abraham Shakespeare. Buddies with old debts to pay or a business idea to nourish got money from him. He gave and gave and gave. It was like Santa Claus had come to Lakeland on a spending binge.

The man who had been a loner for most of his life suddenly found himself with an entourage, with hangers-on accompanying him everywhere he went, soaking up the glory, good fortune, and celebration that enshrouded the former nobody. At bars and nightclubs, women came out of the woodwork to party with the local celeb and, in some cases, seduce him. More than once during the time that she lived with him, Torrie would learn that her boyfriend had ushered another woman home, their comings and goings captured by the security cameras positioned in and around the house. Women he didn't know or barely knew gave him their phone numbers unbidden, and Abraham willingly accepted them. After Torrie moved out, pregnant with Jeremiyah and fed up with Abraham's infidelities, others took their turns with the lothario.

Merely being in Abraham's orbit had its privileges, conveying reflected glory on his posse. Some of his buddies were treated like semi-celebrities in their own rights, and they often used that positioning to woo sexual partners for themselves. They also used it to flex their fledgling power as deal makers and facilitators, like the time one of Abraham's friends introduced Angela Moore to the man of the hour at a local bowling alley.

As their conversation moved past platitudes, Angela shared her dreams of opening a group home in the Lakeland area. She needed $20,000 to make it happen. Abraham, in a fit of grandiosity, offered her twice that amount, but they agreed on $22,200. The next day, Abraham met Angela at her bank to deposit the money.

But while he was freewheeling with loans and gifts to others, Abraham was relatively modest with self-indulgences. His most lavish gift to himself was a lovely, spacious new house in an upscale, gated community on

Redhawk Bend Drive on Lakeland's north side. He paid more than $1 million for the massive, two-story house with four bedrooms, four bathrooms, a pool and spa, and a fireplace. The price also included the furnishings. One real-estate company listing describes the house further:

> The huge gourmet kitchen and breakfast area with Kraftmaid Cabinets, GE Monogram stainless appliances, granite counters opens to the spacious family room featuring a granite faced masonry fireplace and custom coffered wood ceiling. French doors lead to the pool and patio area and the breezeway that connects to the guest suite/4th bedroom with full bath and kitchenette. The master suite is downstairs and also has access to the pool and patio area. The glamour master bath and customized walk in closet are huge. Upstairs is a loft area, 2 bedrooms with walk in closets and a full bath. Custom faux finishes and millwork are evident throughout the home. There are 2 double car garages and ample driveway parking. The screened pool/spa has a paver deck and waterfall feature.

Abraham also bought himself a new pickup truck and a shiny new black BMW 750i, for which he paid a reported $100,000. Considering that Abraham was not known to possess a legal driver's license and, indeed, had gotten into trouble more than once for driving without one, rumors sprang up that Abraham had either paid someone to pretend to be him and take the state license examination or had paid off someone at the Department of Motor Vehicles to issue a license to him. Of course, it was possible that Abraham had actually studied for, taken, and passed the exam on his own, though that was considered improbable since he couldn't read.

It was also possible that he was unconcerned about having a license and was content to drive around without one. Who could sort fact from fiction in the fog of rumor, half-truth, and exaggeration that enveloped Abraham Shakespeare after he won that money?

Barber Greg Smith rejoiced when his old friend showed him the keys to the new house on Redhawk Bend Drive in early January 2007. The two marveled over Abraham's turn in fortune, from homeless to upscale home owner. Greg also couldn't help but notice the big new Rolex on Shakyboy's wrist, and he was happy to learn that his friend had not paid full retail price for the watch but rather had picked it up at a local pawn shop. Greg complimented Abraham on the bargain and wished him well on the Caribbean cruise he was about to embark on with Torrie, the mother of his son, Jeremiyah. Greg hoped the cruise would give Abraham the distance, anonymity, and privacy his friend already achingly wanted.

The relief didn't last long. No sooner had Abraham returned to central Florida from his Caribbean getaway with Torrie than he once again became the community ATM. Fortunately, a friend helped set up some of the handouts as loans rather than as gifts, but chasing people down for their repayments left Abraham feeling worn out and demoralized. His uncle's neighbor, Greg Massey, stepped in to help Abraham maintain his financial records and track down borrowers, often going door-to-door from one debtor to the next, though sometimes collecting more excuses and complaints than payments for his friend.

As if the constant appeals for cash were not enough of an aggravation for a man who was used to going practically unnoticed, Abraham's newfound celebrity also brought more new trouble. Five months after the lottery drawing, Michael Ford, his former meat-delivery partner at MBM, filed a lawsuit claiming that he had purchased the winning lottery ticket for himself and that Abraham had stolen it from him. According to the lawsuit he filed in April 2007, Ford was a frequent visitor at the Frost-proof store that sold the winning ticket and had a habit of buying two tickets, which he then stored in a compartment in the truck.

"Plaintiff did not realize the tickets were missing until Thursday, November 17, 2006 and assumed that he had lost the tickets," read the complaint. "On November 18, 2006, the Plaintiff was informed by his supervisor that Defendant had won the Florida State Lottery that held the drawing on November 15, 2006. On the same day as being advised that the Defendant had won the lottery, Plaintiff confronted the Defendant about the missing lotto tickets from his wallet and was informed by the Defendant that he had removed the tickets from

Plaintiff's wallet, but that Plaintiff could not prove that he had done so." The suit sought injunctive relief—to stop Abraham from spending more money—because "Defendant does not have the ability to replace the losses."

To buttress his client's claims, Ford's attorney, Arnold Levine, made much of Abraham's criminal past, particularly those incidents involving theft.

"Does a leopard change its spots?" he asked. "You have to ask yourself." Levine argued that, without fail, Ford always bought two tickets for himself whenever he visited the store. Therefore, he said, if his client had really purchased two tickets for Abraham, he would have walked out with four tickets that fateful day instead of the two documented by store records. He also insinuated that Abraham had paid witnesses for favorable testimony, in one case, allegedly paying off a man's $185,000 mortgage.

He and Michael Ford had not been particularly close, but Abraham was nonetheless stunned at how his old coworker had turned on him and lied about what happened. Angered by Ford's lawsuit, Abraham hired Valenti, Campbell, Trohn, Tamayo and Aranda, a well-regarded Lakeland law firm, to represent him. But before the case went to trial, he unceremoniously ditched the firm and turned to Willie Gary, a flamboyant and accomplished lawyer from south Florida whose skill, success, and swagger have often been likened to that of the late Johnnie Cochran, of O. J. Simpson "Dream Team" fame. One of eleven children born to migrant farmers in central Georgia, Gary had parlayed his law-school education, gift for gab, doggedness, and supreme confidence into a multimillion-dollar legal empire, replete with corporate jets (including a Boeing 737 named *Wings of Justice II*), and for himself as founding partner, a lavish lifestyle of custom-made suits, Rolls Royces, and mansions. Known in legal circles as "the Giant Killer," Gary had successfully taken on the Walt Disney Corporation—a demigod in Florida—and won a $240 million jury verdict against the enormous corporation for stealing his clients' idea for a sports theme park. He later won a half-billion dollar verdict against a Canadian funeral home chain, which he settled for $175 million, and slew Anheuser-Busch, the world's largest brewery, to the tune of $50 million in a breach-of-contract suit on behalf of the family of the late New York Yankees' great right fielder, Roger Maris, who had gotten into the beer-distribution business.

The trial of *Ford versus Shakespeare* in October 2007, almost a full year after the lotto win, drew standing-room-only crowds eager to get a glimpse of the multimillionaire and to witness the punches and counterpunches they anticipated being thrown by lawyers with known penchants for theatrics and thunder. Deploying his preacher-esque style and appealing to the jurors' common sense, Abraham's lawyer, Willie Gary, argued that Michael Ford's story didn't add up. Why would Abraham steal lotto tickets he had no reason to expect would be worth anything? Gary asked. Besides, Abraham had said that his former coworker had approached him a few days after the win and had asked the newly minted multimillionaire "to help him out" with a million dollars so that Ford could move to

Georgia and start a business. Gary suggested that a robbed man would not ask a favor of his robber.

Despite five days of testimony, the jury took little more than a single hour to reach a verdict in Abraham's favor, an indictment of Ford's poor showing in court.

"I am pleased that justice prevailed and that Mr. Shakespeare was found innocent," Abraham's lawyer said after the verdict. "This lawsuit was about greed. The plaintiff manufactured a story and a plan to try to take advantage of my client."

Though he had won, Abraham was mad as hell at Michael Ford's lawyers for having "scandalized" his name by harping on his criminal record and for effectively arguing that once a crook, always a crook. Still, ever softhearted, he forgave Ford.

"I ain't mad with him. I don't hold it against him," Abraham told reporters who covered the trial. "If he only waited, I could've given him $250,000 easy."

Instead, Michael Ford got nothing but a big dose of national embarrassment and a bill for attorneys' fees. He appealed the case, but the higher court ultimately dismissed the appeal. Financial records show that Abraham paid Willie Gary $800,000 for saving his fortune.

CHAPTER THREE

•••••

While he celebrated his former part-time employee and friend's good fortune, Gregory Todd Smith was struggling with his own money problems. Specifically, the threat of losing his late mother's house to foreclosure was beginning to bear down heavily on Greg. The little house on McDonald Street in Plant City, a small municipality about a dozen miles west of Lakeland and known as the winter strawberry capital of the world, had been the only home his mother, Helen Smith, had ever called her own. As a last gift to her and in honor of the family legacy, Greg and his siblings had vowed to hold on to the property and keep the mortgage, taxes, and insurance current. But as family member after family member suffered financial setbacks, the payments fell behind, and now the bank was threatening to take the house away. Try as they might, Helen's children could not cobble together the tens of thousands of dollars they required to keep the house out of the auctioneer's hands, and time was running out.

The land the house sat on was part of a verdant 700-acre swath of Polk County that had been in the family ever since Greg's late maternal grandfather, the Reverend J. C. Gordon, bought it back in the 1920s, when not many black people in the area could produce a deed in their names. As his children became adults with families of their own, Reverend Gordon divided up the property and built homes for them. Greg's mother was one such beneficiary.

By the time Greg was born, in 1969, the good reverend was well established as a mover and shaker in town, having acquired several plots of land in and around Plant City. In addition to his land holdings, the Reverend Gordon was also known for his carpentry skills and agricultural acumen. His fields yielded rich harvests of vegetables every year, and those crops were reaped (as they had been sown) with the help of the Gordon progeny—children and grandchildren alike—who understood early on that when it came to the old man's crops, they would all have to pitch in. Indeed, most of them began their stints on the farmland at such tender ages that until they were older and wiser, they believed every little child in the world spent his or her days plowing and planting, plucking, and picking.

But school and fieldwork left little time for normal child's play, and eventually, Greg grew to resent the obligation of working on his grandfather's farm, despite the happy camaraderie of siblings and cousins and their grandfather's insistence that the dirty, hot, back-bending labor was teaching them the value of hard work and making them stronger.

At fifteen, just old enough to enter Plant City's summer-employment program for youth, Greg did just that, uncertain what the job entailed but sure that anything was better than being an unpaid or barely paid field hand.

On his first day in the youth program, Greg hopped onto the back of a city truck, along with a troop of other adolescents and teenagers, and watched the city's familiar terrain and landmarks shrink into the horizon as they rode for miles and miles away from Plant City, stopping at last on a long, lonely stretch of highway.

The driver, a chunky, middle-aged white man named Jim, with skin that looked like aged leather, barked the youngsters off of the truck bed and onto the steamy pavement, where each was handed a hoe and instructed to clean up the weeds and debris around the telephone poles that lined the roadway as far as the eye could see.

"And when you're done with this one, move on to the next one," the man said, leaning on a nearby pole and pointing to one farther up the road. "And when you're done with that one, on to the next one and so on and so on till I pick you back up."

"And we're gonna get paid for doing this?" Greg asked Jim.

"Yep, that's the job," he answered.

Although some of the other teenagers bowed their heads fretfully or threatened to walk off the job right then and there, Greg felt relieved. *This is the kind of work I've been doing all my life*, he thought. Only now, he'd actually get paid to do it.

Sure enough, when Jim returned several hours later,

Greg had covered nearly five miles of roadside work. Every telephone pole in his wake sported a fresh pedicure. Greg had even helped some of the other kids tend to their poles, as much out of a sense of competitiveness and ego as to engender a sense of teamwork and solidarity. Granddaddy, taskmaster that he was, had prepared him well. Greg turned out to be one of the best workers the program had ever seen, so much so that the city offered to keep him on part-time even after the program expired as summer came to an end. That made Greg especially proud, since it was the first time in a long time that he had an achievement worth taking home to his grandfather. Greg wanted desperately to get back into his grandfather's good graces. Their relationship had become strained when Greg entered middle school and gained a reputation for being a troublemaker. He'd lost count of how many times he drew detention or was suspended from school, always for fighting. Although a disciplined athlete, Greg had not done much to stem his fiery, quick-trigger temper, and everyone knew it didn't take much to rile him.

"They said I was a behavior problem," Greg later explained. "Not that I had a behavior problem; I *was* a behavior problem."

The pattern of fights and punishments slowed noticeably when Greg made his high school's junior varsity football team. He worked so hard and performed so well that, before the year ended, he was asked to join the varsity squad. Meanwhile, he also was turning heads on the school's track and field team.

Those achievements gave Greg bragging rights both at

home and at school, and, along with the fashionable clothing he was able to buy, thanks to that part-time maintenance job he still had with the city, his talents on the sports fields were gradually turning Greg into a popular standout at Plant City High. Once the girls started batting their eyes at him, stroking his ego and self-confidence, Greg's position as one of the big men on campus was cinched.

With his success in football and track, Greg's temper flare-ups were fewer and farther between, but each time he gave in to them, the school responded with punishments that grew increasingly severe as his athletic prowess and physical maturity made him a more powerful and intimidating force. Greg's recurring scuffles eventually left the school no choice but to expel him.

Being kicked out of school for good dashed Greg's dreams of an athletic scholarship to college, yet he knew there was no way in the world he could leave his education unfinished, not with the Reverend Gordon for a grandfather. Ashamed but determined to redeem himself, Greg promptly signed up for night school to earn his high school diploma. Once he accomplished that, he enrolled in barber college, where he completed the coursework and earned a license to cut hair. A cousin—Derrick Gainer, an NFL running back who'd just gotten drafted by the Oakland Raiders—helped him open his first shop in 1989, in a small plaza on Lakeland's Wabash Avenue, just a few blocks from the national headquarters of Publix Super Markets, the fifth-largest grocery chain in the country.

Though only twenty years old, Greg discerned that empathy and a willing ear were as much in demand by his clientele as a shape up or a shave, so he quickly established his shop as the place to go for a great cut and good conversation.

Before long, his shop also became a transit point for underworld activity. Greg began a fencing operation, buying stolen goods from local thieves at their "discounted" prices, then flipping them for a profit. When even that wasn't enough for the daredevil and hustler in him, he began dabbling in the drug-dealing game. By the summer of 1990, Greg Smith was the man to see for haircuts, conversation, and crack cocaine.

A year later, the cops nabbed Greg on two felony counts for the sale and possession of a controlled substance. At his trial in 1992, Greg was sent to prison for three years, the minimum mandatory under Florida's sentencing guidelines.

Greg left the state correctional facility in 1995, pledging yet another fresh start. His first step was to reestablish his barber business. Having sold the old place just before going off to prison, he soon found a shop on Tenth Street, so he remodeled it and relocated in the hood. That arrangement came to an abrupt end the night Greg was caught hanging out after hours in a part of town known for being a bastion of drug activity, a violation of the curfew prescribed in his terms of parole. The state's attorney wanted to send him back to prison for another fifteen years, but Greg's lawyer was able to get it down to a two-year sentence, which he served without incident.

Determined not to be three times crazy, Greg again rebooted his barber practice in 2001. Two years later, he married Likicha Wilson Laster, a home health-care provider, and the couple settled in Plant City. This time, Greg vowed, he would make his family proud, do right by his grandfather's legacy, and prove that he was self-made and self-reliant.

Greg's blossoming self-esteem and a commitment to do whatever it took for his family was what led him to bite the bullet and, in early 2007, present himself to the MidFlorida Credit Union, where he hoped to arrange a loan to pay off the mortgage company and save his late mother's house. He was reading through the stack of loan documents in his barbershop when Shakyboy walked in.

"What's that, man?" Abraham asked, pointing to the sheaf of papers. "Got your forehead all wrinkled up like you worried."

Greg explained to Abraham that he was about to take out a credit-union loan so that he could salvage the family property. He was going through the documents, line by line, to make sure he knew what he was getting into, he said.

"Why you didn't ask me for the money?" Abraham asked, hurtfully.

"Boy, you got every Tom, Dick, and Harry within a hundred miles asking you for money," said Greg. "That's your money. I'm not trying to be another one of those folks running up on you for a handout."

Abraham's expression grew stern. As Greg's friend,

he said, he would be a fairer lender than any credit union. He scolded Greg for not coming to him first.

"Man, I appreciate that, but I'm good here," Greg said. "All I got to do is sign these papers, and it's on. But I thank you, man, but you got enough niggas out here dipping in your pocket."

Abraham left but returned to the shop a few hours later with a cashier's check for sixty-three thousand dollars made out to Gregory Todd Smith, declaring that he would not sit by and watch his old friend get ripped off by some bank when he—his friend—had the means to help.

Touched by Abraham's generosity and surprised by his insistence, Greg studied the cashier's check in disbelief.

"Well, I guess we got a deal then," he said.

"You can tear them papers up," Abraham replied, indicating the credit-union documents.

The men agreed that Greg would pay Shakyboy five hundred and forty dollars a month until the sixty-three thousand dollars had been repaid in full. The property on McDonald Street would serve as collateral. Abraham would have Greg Massey drop off the papers for Greg to sign and seal the deal.

The next month, Greg Smith counted out five hundred and forty dollars, then added nearly twenty-five hundred dollars more, folded the bills, put a rubber band around them and handed the wad of cash over to Abraham. By paying the agreed-upon installment nearly six times over, Greg wanted to prove that he was not like the deadbeats who'd taken Abraham's money only to vanish at collection time. Month in and month out,

Greg would give either Abraham or Greg Massey three thousand dollars in cash and collect a receipt.

One afternoon in early 2009, Shakyboy pulled up to Greg's barbershop in his big pretty BMW. Through the shop window, Greg could see a woman in the car's front passenger seat. *That must be the chick Abraham was talking about, the one who's gonna be handling his business,* Greg thought. Earlier that day, Abraham had called Greg to tell him about a "white lady" who was going to be helping him manage his financial affairs, including the collection of loan payments.

Abraham walked into the shop and, sure enough, said to Greg, "I want you to come out and meet the lady we talked about."

Greg put down his clippers and excused himself from the shop, running his hands over his closely-shaven head and then smoothing the hairs of his impeccably trimmed goatee. He swiftly whisked away any stray hairs or powder from his T-shirt and jeans. Greg prided himself on his neat and clean appearance, and was happy that, even nearing forty, he was still as slender and fit as he had been in high school. If Abraham was bringing someone around to impress him, Greg figured he should do some impressing of his own.

As he and Abraham exited the shop, the woman in the passenger seat got out of the car and met them on the sidewalk.

"This here is Dee Dee Moore," Abraham said, standing between the two strangers. "I just wanted y'all to know each other."

CHAPTER FOUR

•••••

The big blonde woman standing beside Abraham Shakespeare looked uneasy and out of place. Her weak, quivering smile betrayed discomfort, and although six feet tall—standing shoulder to shoulder with Abraham but several inches taller than Greg—she appeared shy and cowering. When Greg Smith extended his hand to shake hers, she met it with a brief, clammy half grip. Greg tried to maintain eye contact with her, but the woman kept looking away, either at Abraham or at nearby shops. Greg found her meekness unbecoming in someone who was supposed to be a business whiz. What he saw that day seemed more shrinking violet than financial guru.

Despite his initial impression, however, Greg would come to learn that Dee Dee Moore was no pushover. Far from it. Beneath the surface of her meek exterior lay an enormous capacity for brazenness, audacity, and connivance, all traits that Dee Dee had repeatedly, and often successfully, deployed throughout her adult life to get out of binds or to take advantage of something—or someone.

Scandal was in the air on July 25, 1972, the day Dorice Emma Donegan was born to Linda and Patrick Donegan. Newspapers heralded an Associated Press exposé of the infamous Tuskegee Experiment, the U.S. government's pretense of giving free treatment to poor, black men in Alabama who had syphilis when, in fact, officials had only offered placebos to the men, whom they tracked for forty years to see what happened when the disease was left unattended. This sordid saga of calculated deception, disregard, and exploitation of poor, black men was all the news when Dee Dee Donegan arrived.

Her childhood began in a small house on the invitingly named Happy Acres Lane, in Riverview, Florida, and continued on Turkey Creek Road, in Plant City, where the family moved when Dee Dee was seven years old. Linda Donegan recalls her daughter's childhood as "gleeful" and normal. Dee Dee belonged to a Brownie troop, then became a Girl Scout. She joined a Bible study group called the Missionettes and regularly attended church—every Wednesday and Sunday, according to Linda. At her elementary school, Dee Dee was a cheerleader. In high school, she joined the ROTC. She was outgoing and ambitious and a word frequently used to sum up her personality was *bubbly*.

It was in high school, however, that Dee Dee apparently first decided that the modest existence her parents provided was not for her. When she entered Plant City

High School, Dee Dee seemed painfully aware of class divisions—the haves and the have-nots—and would insist that her parents drop her off a block away from friends' houses or other meeting spots because she was embarrassed by the family car. She craved fashionable clothes, cars, jewelry, and other luxuries unattainable on her parents' wages from their work as a nursing assistant and an air-conditioning serviceman. "We didn't have much money," Linda says, recalling her daughter's shame.

After graduating high school, Dee Dee earned her own certification as a nursing assistant, like her mother, and, now nineteen years old, went to work. She was said to be good at her job and was considered generous and kind to her patients, especially the developmentally disabled.

Two months shy of her twentieth birthday, Dee Dee married James Darrel Moore of nearby Dover, Florida. James was a stocky, dark-haired man who worked with his father in the excavation business, running heavy equipment. The newlyweds lived in a trailer on his parents' property. Two and a half years later, Dee Dee gave birth to a son whom she and her husband named Robert James and whom the family called R. J.

Tragedy struck in 1995, when twenty-two-year-old Dee Dee was driving a Hummer on State Road 33 late one evening and a Pontiac Sunfire crossed the center line and crashed into her head-on. A passenger in the small car, a woman around Dee Dee's age, died that night. The Pontiac's seventeen-year-old driver died the next day. Dee Dee was briefly hospitalized, but her injuries were never life-threatening and she recovered fully, although, in years to come, her mother would sometimes wonder if Dee Dee's often erratic behavior was the result of an undetected brain injury suffered that night.

Always on the lookout for an opportunity to enrich her bank account, Dee Dee added a sideline to her work as a certified nursing assistant. She began selling prepaid phones and calling plans for a wireless company. The extra income allowed her to buy some of the niceties for herself and her family that had been unaffordable in her youth.

Karen DiSalvo, who worked for Arcadia Healthcare in Tampa as a registered nurse and office manager, remembered when Dee Dee came to work at the medical staffing company as a certified nurse's assistant in the early 1990s. She described her as ambitious and outgoing, with a seemingly natural acumen for the business and administrative aspects, traits that got her noticed by the higher-ups. Karen liked the up-and-comer and trusted her business savvy so much that she and her husband began partnering with Dee Dee to open a sideline business selling cell phones and services, with their fellow employees at Arcadia as a customer base. In 2004, they incorporated a business called All About Cellular, with Karen listed as president and Dee Dee as vice president, but the partnership with the DiSalvos stalled when Dee Dee became preoccupied with opening a new Arcadia Healthcare branch in Plant City, having convinced her bosses that the town was an untapped gold mine.

According to Karen, Dee Dee hadn't been at the new location long before staff began noticing a decided spike in spending. A subsequent internal investigation revealed that Dee Dee, who had check-writing authority, had skimmed sixty thousand dollars off the payroll. Karen told detectives the probe showed that Dee Dee padded checks to some employees and collected the difference between what the workers were really owed and the higher check amount, sometimes splitting the windfall with the employee. Just as Arcadia was beginning legal action against Dee Dee, the Plant City branch burned down—but only files were lost. Expensive equipment just happened to have been moved to a neighboring business. According to Karen, eventually Dee Dee and Arcadia settled their differences for twenty-five thousand dollars, but Karen suspected that Dee Dee never paid.

In 1999, when she was twenty-seven, Dee Dee was charged with shoplifting in Polk County. She got probation. Two years later, she and her husband, James, fell severely behind on their rent for a house they were leasing in Dover. Dee Dee told her landlords that someone was after her and that she had found a blazing "warning sign" on her front porch. Despite this tale of woe, the Moore family was eventually evicted. Later that year, 2001, Dee Dee was arrested for writing a bad check for $418 to the Hillsborough County tax collector. As with the shoplifting charge, she was sentenced to probation and fined for the bad check but served no jail time. Then she stepped into darker waters.

In June 2001, the credit union that had financed Dee Dee's $50,000 Lincoln Navigator was threatening repossession after several missed car loan payments. When her usual excuses did not satisfy the lender or buy her more time, Dee Dee defiantly announced to the loan officer who had called her about the repossession that she would "do anything I have to" to keep the luxury sports-utility vehicle. Days later, a bizarre string of events unfolded.

A motorist in Wimauma, a little town about forty miles away from Dee Dee's home in Plant City, found a disheveled and distraught woman alongside a county road with her wrists bound. He took her to the police, where the victim reported that three clean-cut, tattooed Hispanic men had abducted and raped her at gunpoint, thrown her into a ditch, and stolen her car, a Lincoln Navigator.

"The one in back finally made the decision not to kill me but said he better never see me again and to dye my hair blonde," she told police. Asked about details of the assault, Dee Dee Moore broke down in front of investigators. "If I describe that, I'm gonna start crying and throwing up again," she said. "They, um, had sex with me. And it hurt." Naturally, the new Hillsborough County case included a lookout for the stolen vehicle in hopes of locating Dee Dee's alleged assailants. As the *Tampa Bay Times* later reported, "Detectives took her pink sweater, blue jeans, bra, underwear, and fingernail scrapings into evidence. They would soon learn from a Nextel representative that Moore had been banned from selling the phone company's products due to an internal fraud investigation."

A few days later, a man in a neighboring county called police to say that he had seen Dee Dee's story on the local news. The Navigator, he said, was in the garage of his home. Another man had driven the car to his garage, he said. A second man later confessed to being the driver, telling police that Dee Dee had told him she wanted to frame a former coworker at the cell phone company who had snitched on her and gotten her banned from selling the company's products on suspicion of fraud. Yet a third man told police that he was the one who drove Dee Dee out to Wimauma so that someone could discover her bound and gagged. He said Dee Dee had taped her own wrists and, spotting a ditch along the road, had ordered him to slow down and then thrown herself from his SUV.

For all of that, Dee Dee got a year of probation. And lost the Navigator.

In 2006, a husband and wife accused Dee Dee of making off with $60,000 they had given her to deposit into a payroll account for a new business she'd helped them set up. The wife had worked for American Medical Professionals (AMP), a medical staffing agency that Dee Dee had incorporated earlier that year. Dee Dee admitted that she had not made the deposit but claimed the money had been hers to keep. The case was closed for lack of evidence.

"She tells the fibbiest fibs," Patrick Donegan would later say of his daughter. He recalled the suspicious fire at the Arcadia office in Plant City, noting that no one had been hurt and that everything of any real use and value to Dee Dee had been spared, a blessing he found "strange."

"Sometimes I shake my head," Patrick said of his daughter's questionable actions.

At least two businesses filed civil lawsuits against Dee Dee, one for $3,600 in back office rent; another for $20,700 in unpaid radio advertising. Clearly, she lived by the skin of her teeth. And dined on melodrama and bathos.

Yet for all of Dee Dee's shadiness and criminality, all the loss of credibility and trust with her employers, friends and family, all the close calls, crime had not paid. But it hadn't cost her either. Being the inveterate hustler that she was, Dee Dee kept both her freedom and her ambitions intact.

When she'd opened American Medical Professionals, in 2006, one of her first employees was Patricia Paulson, the former director of nurses at Conway Lakes Nursing Home in Orlando. In that capacity, Patricia had hired Dee Dee a few times when she needed an extra certified nursing assistant for the patients. They struck up a friendship and, when AMP launched, Dee Dee brought Patricia on as a substitute nurse.

It was then that the thirty-four-year-old Dee Dee met Patricia's son, Shar, a blue-eyed, caramel-haired, slightly built twenty-three-year-old charmer with two years of community college under his belt but no job. Despite the eleven-year age difference, their friendship quickly turned to romance.

Separated from James, Dee Dee invited Shar to move in with her and R. J., a proposition the jobless young man took her up on in January 2007. Right away, Dee Dee set about to impress Shar, making him an officer in her company and supplying him with free housing, expensive clothes, and lavish vacations. In 2008, she rented a split-level house out on State Road 60 East in Plant City and set up her business offices there, allowing Shar's mother, Patricia, to live in the house rent-free. The next year, she bought the house next door, telling Shar that she paid for it with $300,000 the IRS had paid her for turning in deadbeat taxpayers. It was the second time she'd gotten paid six figures for whistle-blowing to the IRS, she told him. For all Shar knew, Dee Dee Moore was every bit the successful business woman she claimed to be. Whatever the true state of Dee Dee's financial affairs, one thing Shar knew for sure was that he was enjoying the good life, free of charge. By the spring of 2009, he and Dee Dee were even living in a big, pricey new house in one of Lakeland's premier communities, and he was sporting around in a shiny new Corvette with a Rolex watch on his arm.

Barbara Jackson couldn't believe it when Dee Dee pulled up to the Red Lobster in Lakeland in October 2008 and bounded out of her SUV wearing a snazzy dress and high heels. Barbara and Dee Dee had met less than two weeks earlier at a small business conference in central Florida, and at the time, Dee Dee had been moving about in a wheelchair, seemingly pained and purportedly disabled from what she said was a recent vehicle accident. Barbara hadn't expected to see that same woman looking so hardy and spry so soon.

"Scuba therapy," was how Dee Dee explained her hastened recovery. Scuba therapy?

Barbara Jackson was a real-estate agent, and she had participated in a panel discussion at the conference, where she spoke of meeting a downtrodden man who had hit the Florida lottery and brokered the deal that got him a fancy new house in Lakeland. Barbara told the conferees that the man had been extraordinarily generous with his winnings and that his kindness had changed her thinking about the purpose of money. She now believed it was only as valuable as the amount of joy and satisfaction it could bring and that merely having a lot of it was not an end unto itself, she said. Dee Dee had lit up at the real-estate agent's message.

"I need to meet this man," Dee Dee told Barbara afterward. "I'm a writer, and I would love to tell his story in a magazine article, maybe even a book."

Barbara had set up the introduction soon thereafter, and once the formalities were dispensed, Dee Dee began charming and dazzling Abraham with promises of writing a positive article—something that would exalt him as a productive and generous man, adjectives he had never before heard connected to his name or reputation. Over the next few weeks, Abraham saw a lot of Dee Dee, and although the article never materialized, she quite obviously won his trust. By the time January 2009 rolled around, Abraham had replaced Greg Massey with Dee Dee Moore as his helpmate, collector, and advisor on financial matters.

From the start, Greg Massey and others had a bad feeling about Dee Dee, this Johnny-come-lately, and they had vigorously argued their misgivings to Abraham. But

Shakyboy would have none of it, and, according to Massey, the two parted ways when Abraham insisted on entrusting his affairs to the burly blonde.

Greg Smith had known about Abraham's falling out with Greg Massey and had heard that Shakyboy was tooling around town with an unfamiliar white woman. Now here they were at his shop. Even though Abraham had told him they were coming by, Greg could not help but stare at the strange sight. For one thing, Shakyboy had never been known to have any intentional dealings with white people. Everyone knew Abraham didn't particularly like them; he damn sure didn't trust them.

Although Abraham had apparently made an exception for Dee Dee Moore, there was something about the woman that set off Greg's mental alarms on first sighting. *She don't look like no accountant*, he thought. *She ain't got no briefcase with her, no folders or papers. She don't look like she's handling business.*

"Hey, I ain't trying to get in your business," Greg had cautioned Shakyboy earlier that day, when Abraham called to say he and his new advisor were going to stop by. "Man, just be careful."

He had felt a little bad afterward for having openly questioned another grown man's decision and, perhaps, having planted some seeds of worry and doubt in Abraham's already troubled mind. But now that he saw Dee Dee for himself, Greg wished he had challenged Shakyboy's decision much more strenuously.

He might have been even more aggressive had he known just how deeply into Abraham's pockets this strange woman had already gotten. By the time she and Greg were introduced, Dee Dee was in the process of taking control over all of Abraham's assets—cash, collectible loans, and property. She had convinced him that it was not only the most efficient way to manage his affairs, but that it would insulate him from borrowers, bill and tax collectors, and the mothers of his children, especially Torrie, who was seeking a court order for child support. Abraham had signed over to Dee Dee's company the deeds to not only two small houses that he owned after foreclosing on unpaid loans, but also title to the house he had so proudly purchased on Redhawk Bend Drive. Abraham had also signed an asset-purchase agreement that gave Dee Dee's company, AMP, ownership of five outstanding loans that were collateralized with houses valued at nearly $400,000. That included Greg's loan, which was secured by his late mother's house.

Had Greg known that Dee Dee was more than just Abraham's helper, more than just his loan-payment collector, he would have done all he could to make Abraham cut his ties with the woman. He couldn't have known then that he wouldn't get another chance to hold court with Abraham. He couldn't have known then that it was the last time he would see his old friend.

CHAPTER FIVE

•••••

Greg Smith got his first call from Dee Dee Moore early in the afternoon on a Saturday about three weeks after he was introduced to her. She told him that she would be stopping by his shop later that day to collect that month's loan installment. But Greg didn't want Dee Dee in his shop because it would set too many tongues wagging. He agreed to call her when he was closing up for the day so they could rendezvous at a local supermarket before he headed home.

The exchange was quick and without incident, except that Dee Dee did not produce a receipt, which Abraham or Greg Massey had unfailingly provided. *This is not the way to start off*, Greg thought, insisting that Dee Dee get a receipt to him right away.

"I'll get it to you tomorrow; no problem," she said.

First thing the next day, Greg called Dee Dee to inquire

about his receipt but got no answer. He called again, and again got no response. The next time he called, Greg left a voice-mail message. Hours passed before Dee Dee called back, telling him she was on her way over to Greg's shop with the receipt. She never showed up.

"Listen, I got your money," Greg said to Dee Dee when she called the next month to set up the payment exchange. "But, hey, I can't give you no money with no receipt. Now I need both receipts for last month and this new payment." Greg had heard that Abraham was out of town and told Dee Dee that he wanted to make sure Shakyboy knew he was being repaid as expected.

He was relieved when, at that day's meeting, and at the next one a month later, Dee Dee provided handwritten receipts for each $3,000 cash payment. Because she had made good on those transactions, Greg's reservations about Abraham's emissary began to fade. *After all*, he thought, *what do I care if Shakyboy wants to let this woman handle things for him? All I've got to do is see her for five minutes once a month.*

But his worries about Dee Dee returned with a vengeance when the day's mail brought a disturbing letter notifying him that American Medical Professionals, Dee Dee's medical staffing company, was contemplating foreclosure proceedings against him, citing failure to make payments on the loan collateralized by the house Greg was so determined to keep in the family. He put in a frantic and angry call to Dee Dee.

"Call me," he demanded. "I need to talk to you about a letter I just got." Messing with his money had always been a trigger point for Greg, especially when he knew that not only had he been holding up his end of the bargain, he'd been exceeding it. He felt like steam was rising from his head as he read the letter over and over in disbelief, waiting for his phone to ring.

Over the next couple of hours, Greg placed three more calls to Dee Dee's cell phone, each time getting her voice mail and never a return call. He had not wanted to disturb Abraham, who Dee Dee had said was away on a cruise, but Greg now felt he had no choice and dialed the familiar number. When Abraham didn't pick up, Greg left a voice mail.

"Shakyboy, man, I know you're on vacation, man. I know you're trying to relax some damn where. You're probably getting you a shot of ass or something," Greg said, feigning calm. "But they're saying they're going to foreclose on my property like I ain't been paying you and you know I have. I need to talk to you, man."

While he waited for a call back, Greg called Judy Haggins, another old friend of Abraham's who used to hang out with him in local clubs. Greg knew that Judy was something of an errand-runner for Abraham and that, if anyone knew how to reach him, she would. He had no idea when he placed the call that Shakyboy had given Judy power of attorney over his holdings at the urging of Dee Dee Moore, who convinced Abraham that conferring that authority on someone he knew and trusted would free him from the tedium of signing papers, attending meetings, and handling other mundane business matters. That way, she told Abraham, if he wanted or needed to be away, someone else would be able to keep his affairs in order. The papers prepared by Dee Dee's lawyer, Howard Stitzel, were duly signed and notarized in Lakeland on April 3, 2009.

Vested with authority she did not understand, Judy put herself at Dee Dee's beck and call and simply waited for direction from the conductor of Abraham's affairs. When she wasn't meeting Dee Dee at a bank or other place of business to sign a document in Abraham's stead, Judy busied herself with driving Abraham's mother to and from work, running errands for Dee Dee, or helping make the rounds of loan-payment collections from the many people indebted to Abraham.

Greg found it ridiculous when Judy told him that she had Abraham's power of attorney. He knew her as an unaccomplished party girl with no particular skills, and if she had any smarts about business or legal matters, it was certainly news to him. He considered the move another bad decision by Abraham, but he decided that if Shakyboy was happy with it, so be it, because it was for sure none of his business. Dispensing with courtesies, he huffily told Judy about the foreclosure threat and got straight to the point.

"Where's my damn money?" Greg shouted through the phone. "They saying I haven't made my payments or haven't made them on time when, to tell you the truth, I'm ahead because I was only supposed to pay $540 a month and I've been paying $3,000 because I wanted to get this shit over with. So, where's my money going? Y'all talking about I'm going into foreclosure. I'm waiting for Abraham to call me back."

"Abe's in Texas," Judy said. "I just went to see him."

"Whatever," Greg said. "I just know I called that Dee Dee heffa four or five times, and she ain't called me back. I better hear from her by tomorrow morning or I'm going to go find her ass."

The foreclosure letter was a mistake, Judy assured him. "It's all been taken care of."

"Then I want papers—signed papers—saying that it's okay. Tell Dee Dee Moore I need to talk to her about my papers. I'm gonna tell Shakyboy about this when he calls me back, too."

"He's only dealing with text messages," Judy said. "I'll make sure Dee Dee gets in touch with you right away."

Hours passed with no return call from either Abraham or Dee Dee. Finally, frustrated, Greg decided to send Abraham a text, though it struck him as a strange way to reach a man so estranged from the written word. In all the years Greg had known Abraham, they had never talked by text message; it had always been either face-to-face or by phone. Still, Greg picked up his phone and began typing out a text to Abraham: "Man, call my fucking phone. This cracka has got my damn money and I know if you get this message, you gone call me before I whip this cracka's ass about my damn money." A second text from Greg read, simply, "Call me. It's important."

"Bro, I'm on a cruise and I'll be back in town soon," read the text message from Abraham Shakespeare's phone. "I just needed to get away because all these niggers are bothering me about money."

Greg reeled. As peculiar as it had been for him to text

Abraham, it was even stranger to get a text message back, given that Abraham could barely read or write. Greg was dumbfounded that his old friend was suddenly not only writing messages, but oddly formal-sounding ones, no less. And "these niggers"? What was up with that? No real black man said "niggers." It was "niggas" or "niggaz."

Doubts aside, Greg wrote back. "Dawg, I understand that, but this is me. Call my phone. Call me now."

"I'll call you in the morning," read the response. "I'm just trying to get myself together."

Unease nagged at Greg all night. It just didn't make sense for Abraham to respond by text message rather than by simply picking up the phone and calling him, as he had done countless times over the years. When Greg told his wife that night about the exchange, she too was surprised to hear that Abraham had texted her husband. Greg showed her the messages. "That doesn't sound like him," she agreed.

"Tell you what," Greg said to Likicha. "Why don't you send a text to Abraham from your phone?"

"What do you want me to say?"

"Just something short and sweet. Like 'I miss you, baby. When you coming home?'"

Entering Abraham's number, Likicha slowly typed in a text. "Baby, I love you," it said. "Would you please come home?"

Moments later the telltale chime of a text came through. Abraham had responded.

"I'll be home soon and I'll call you when I get back," the text read.

"Something's not right," Greg said. "I know Abraham. That ain't him. And Abraham ain't letting nobody get that telephone and text back with no woman for him."

The next day was well underway, and Greg had still not heard from Dee Dee about the documentation he needed to put the threat of foreclosure to rest. Fuming, he picked up his cell phone and dialed Judy.

"Where the fuck is Dee Dee Moore?" Greg thundered into the phone. "Tell her she needs to come contact me now."

"Dee Dee wants to meet," Judy said sheepishly. "She has the papers that show everything has been taken care of and refinanced."

"I don't know anything about refinancing, but okay. Tell her let's meet," Greg said.

A subsequent call from Judy brought quick relief to Greg's rattled mind. She said she was going to meet Abraham and Dee Dee that evening at the Hard Rock casino in Tampa, a half hour's drive from Lakeland. If Greg could show up, she was sure they could clear the air about the loan and foreclosure threat once and for all.

"Okay, but I'm going to have to act like I don't have anything to do with you," Greg said. "Dee Dee don't need to know you and me been talking 'cause she'll think we don't trust her and are scheming against her. Best to keep me out of the middle as far as she's concerned." Judy agreed.

It was an early April evening. The kind of night that

gives central Florida its allure. Temperatures were in the eighties, the humidity was low, and a constant light breeze tickled the spring air. Pulling into the hotel and casino compound, Greg circled the parking lot to see if he could spot either Dee Dee's or Abraham's vehicles. He had tried to reach Judy earlier to confirm that the plan was still on, but she hadn't answered the call, leading Greg to believe that the party was already situated in the noisy casino. But there was no sign of any of them. Greg pulled into a parking spot and waited until his patience ran out, and he went inside to look around. Nothing. No Abraham, no Judy, no Dee Dee anywhere to be found. Exasperated, he dialed Judy's number again. This time she answered.

"Where are you?" Greg asked. "I'm at the casino."

"I'm not at the casino yet," Judy said. "But Dee Dee's s'posed to be there with her boyfriend. Walk around and see if you can find them."

"I told you I'm at the casino. I already walked all through here. I don't know the boyfriend, but I know Dee Dee and she's not here. I'm gonna call her phone now."

Dee Dee did not answer Greg's call, so he called Judy again.

"I called Dee Dee but she isn't answering," he said. "I don't know what's going on, but I ain't got time for this runaround shit. All I know is y'all better get this shit together. I'm going back home."

"I don't know what's going on either, but I'm gonna try to find out what happened," Judy said. "I'll talk to you tomorrow."

Greg tossed and turned all night, battling a sinking feeling that his business deal with Abraham—and perhaps Abraham himself—was on the skids.

The next morning, he called Judy again. "What the fuck is going on?" Greg demanded. "Why wasn't anybody at the casino? You think something has happened to Abraham?"

"Well," said Judy, "Something did kind of happen to Abraham."

"What you mean?"

"Well, I got to the casino, but Dee Dee called me to leave and come meet her and another white woman on Highway 60. Abraham was in the backseat. He was bleeding. He had cut his arm. Dee Dee said they were taking him to the hospital."

"Whaaaat?"

"Dee Dee said Abraham got into it with some girl, a prostitute who was real young, and they got into some kind of fight or something. The girl was going to the hospital too, but Dee Dee and this other white lady wanted to get Abraham to the hospital so that's why they weren't at the casino."

The story didn't sound right at all to Greg. But, considering Abraham's indiscriminate history with women, it was not impossible that something with a strange lady had gone terribly awry. One thing was for sure, he thought; things are not going well for Abraham. But what was this about Dee Dee and another white woman taking Abraham to the hospital? What "other white lady"?

"Man, this some shit," he said.

"I know."

"Why didn't you call somebody?"

"Abraham doesn't want anyone to know he's back in town."

"Why didn't you call me?"

"It was an emergency and I didn't know what to do."

Two more confusion- and frustration-filled days passed before Greg picked up his phone to finally see Dee Dee Moore's name on an incoming call. She told him that she was calling to assure him that the foreclosure was off, there had been a mistake in the paperwork, and that her lawyers had prepared documents to correct it. Greg and Dee Dee agreed to meet the next day at his mother's house in Plant City—the same house he was struggling to save and working to restore. This time, Dee Dee actually showed up, arriving in the gray Hummer she had bought not long after meeting Abraham. Her disheveled hair was tied back in a ponytail that slithered down her back. Her jeans and shirt were dirty, and her old, heavy boots were covered in what looked like dust.

"Ahh, the infamous Dee Dee Moore," Greg said as his visitor stepped into the house.

"Why are you saying that?" Dee Dee asked, coyly. "Don't look at me, I've been hanging drywall at my house all day."

Greg let it slide. No need to cry over the spilled milk

of unanswered urgent calls. He didn't even want to get started on the casino fiasco especially since, as far as she knew, he was unaware of the drama. Any reference to the Hard Rock fiasco would betray his connection to Judy, and he didn't want Dee Dee to know the two were talking. Greg chose to stick to the business at hand.

"I need to get this paperwork, and I need to talk to Abraham," Greg said, dispensing with small talk. "Where is he?" Greg pulled a chair down from a stack of furniture so Dee Dee could have a seat.

"Oh, Abraham is fine," Dee Dee said, with a wave of her hand. "He just left on another trip. I just talked to him. Everything's fine. I got the paperwork straight and all. I'm really sorry about this. It was just a mistake."

Greg was relieved to hear from the woman in charge that he was no longer in danger of losing his mother's house. There were a few more questions he needed answered, but Dee Dee abruptly dropped the subject.

"Ooh, this is great what you're doing to the house," she cooed. "I'm really impressed. Maybe you can do some work on some of my houses. They need some help."

Greg didn't know what houses Dee Dee was talking about or how many there were, but he would talk about possible restoration jobs later. Right now, he wanted to get this foreclosure mess put to rest, and he wanted to talk to Abraham, just to affirm Dee Dee's assurances.

"When I got that letter, I tried to reach Abraham, but couldn't get him," Greg said, pulling his cell phone from his pocket and scrolling through old texts. "Look here at this text I got from him." Greg stared at Dee Dee as she scanned the small screen. "I never got a text from him before."

"Aww, you're so sweet to check on him," Dee Dee said, smiling. "Most people don't." She explained that Abraham had a new lady friend who was writing his texts for him. "He's going to classes, learning to read and write."

"Okay, then," Greg said, in no mood for a cockamamie story about Abraham taking time on his cruise for literacy lessons. "Just give me the paperwork to show my lawyer."

The document, prepared by Howard Stitzel, the same lawyer who drew up the power of attorney documents, indeed declared that the house on McDonald Street was not in danger of foreclosure and that Greg was not in arrears in his loan payments. The document was just what Greg had hoped for, but it was not enough to quash all of his uneasiness with the woman who had, for days, clearly been dodging his calls. He told Dee Dee he wanted his own lawyer to look over the paperwork before they both signed it.

Greg was in his barbershop the next day when Judy called, asking if Greg could meet with her and Dee Dee to finalize the documents about the foreclosure. He was happy to oblige and took some comfort in the fact that, this time, Dee Dee and Judy had reached out to him, rather than put him through another cat-and-mouse game.

Not five minutes had passed before Judy called back to announce that she and Dee Dee had arrived and were waiting in the car outside Greg's shop.

Just beyond the barbershop door sat a sparkling new, jet-black 2009 Hummer. Judy Haggins was in the front seat, passenger's side. Behind the wheel was Dee Dee Moore, her reddened face streaked with tears and mascara.

"Can you get in and take a ride with us?" Dee Dee whimpered between sniffles.

Immediately, Greg's gut warned him against getting into a vehicle with a distraught white woman that he barely knew and didn't trust, but before he could obey the feeling, Greg opened the back door and plopped into the Hummer's backseat. Dee Dee sped off, turning the corner, and pulling into a Home Depot parking lot, where she came to an abrupt stop and burst into tears.

"Oh, Greg. I got so much stress on me," she wailed. "I don't know why these people think I did something to Abraham."

"Did something to Abraham?" Greg asked. "What you mean?"

"You haven't heard people saying I did something to Abraham?"

"All I heard is that Abraham gone on a trip somewhere."

"Right. And I just wish he would bring his ass back so I can get my life back."

By now, Greg's gut was coming through loud and clear. *Get out of this car, now.*

"Look, I'm sure Abraham will be back soon and you

can get all this cleared up," Greg said, determined to get Dee Dee calmed down so he could make a safe exit. "Fuck what people say. They don't know. Right now, though, I've got to get back to my business." He didn't exhale until the Hummer pulled up in front of his shop and he stepped out. "Check you later," he said, as Dee Dee drove off, seemingly soothed.

CHAPTER SIX

· · · · ·

Greg Smith had not been the only one recently receiving unusual texts from Abraham Shakespeare, nor was he the only one who found them suspicious.

Never once had Antoinette Andrews, Moses's mother, communicated with her child's father by text until the summer of 2009, when she suddenly received several text messages from Abraham's phone in lieu of phone calls or visits. Likewise, Linnette Williams, Abraham's "godsister," said she too received a slew of texts from him, as many as sixty. Linnette was perplexed by Abraham's sudden proclivity for text messaging but happy to learn that he was alright. It helped when Judy Haggins told her the same story she'd told Greg about having visited Abraham in Texas.

Papi Zaid, who had taken out four loans totaling $1 million from Abraham, would much later tell investigators he got a detailed text about his account, along with Abraham's assertion that he was "fine." In addition, Abraham's nephew, James Jr., received several "I'm okay" texts, as did Ashley McMillian, Abraham's stepsister, the daughter of his mother's ex-husband. After hitting the lottery, Abraham had gifted Ashley's father, Arthur Parker, with a million dollars, and he'd given large amounts to Ashley and her sister as well. Though divorce had severed their legal relationship, the McMillians had all remained close with Abraham and had tried to keep in touch. In one text exchange, Ashley had asked Abraham where he was and when he planned to return home. She was flabbergasted when he texted back that he was "a grown ass man" who would come back when he was good and ready. Ashley was certain that Abraham would never say something like that to her. Greg Massey, Abraham's former business associate, became immediately suspicious when a text from Abraham appeared on his phone, so he responded with a question only Abraham could answer. Greg Massey never heard back.

Aside from their incredulity over his apparent decision to stop communicating except via uncharacteristic text messaging, Abraham's increasingly suspicious friends and relatives had one other unsettling thing in common: none of them had seen or spoken to him since early April 2009.

It was autumn now, and the eleven-mile corridor between Lakeland and Plant City was abuzz with gossip and innuendo about Abraham Shakespeare, his money, and the white woman who had taken over his business affairs. The story that he was away on vacation—talk that had begun in the spring—had long ago run its course. Now other rumors were afloat.

Abraham was in Puerto Rico on a business deal.

He had moved to another Florida city to an unknown address with an unnamed woman.

He was in Jamaica getting treatment for AIDS.

Someone had seen him in Texas; someone else had seen him in New Orleans.

Some said he was dodging the endless stream of supplicants who came asking for money.

Others said he was trying to avoid child-support enforcement for Jeremiah.

Another story was that Abraham had gotten hooked on dope and was wasting away in some obscure hovel in south Florida, a story that his lifelong friend Theodore Day found especially preposterous since he had never known Abraham to even toy with drugs, let alone abuse them. Yet another tale had Abraham on the run after having assaulted an underage prostitute, the story advanced by Dee Dee after the Hard Rock casino no-show.

Worried relatives pressed Abraham's mother, Elizabeth Walker, to file a missing-person's report on her son. Arthur Parker, his former stepfather, even tried to file the report himself but was rebuffed by the Lakeland Police Department because he did not have the familial authority to declare Abraham missing.

Cedric Edom, a close cousin of Abraham's, had discouraged the filing of a missing-person's report and went to great lengths to assure his Aunt Elizabeth that he'd spoken to Abraham by phone almost every day and that her son was planning to return to the Lakeland area soon, certainly by the approaching holiday season. Back in August, Cedric had delivered an envelope to his aunt containing a birthday card, a Christian cross pendant, and $100 cash. A note scribbled on the card promised that "I'll be home soon." Although Cedric never said where he got the package, he did not object when Elizabeth Walker said the signature on the card appeared to be her son's scribbled penmanship. For a while after that, the rumors died down. If the man's mother said she had heard from him, then good enough.

By November 2009, however, Abraham had been absent for too long to ignore. One person who could not shake the bad feeling about Abraham that had been gnawing at her for months was Essie Black. Abraham was like a son to her, and it was unlike him to go away without telling her, let alone to stay away for so long with no word. For months, there had been no phone calls, no visits, no letters, no anything. Not even at tax-filing time, when she invariably heard from him, since she was the one who'd prepared his tax returns each year since Abraham won the lottery.

In early November 2009, the elderly woman had decided that even if the rumors were true that Abraham had skipped town to avoid being hassled by borrowers and baby mamas and child-support-enforcement folks, people who cared about him deserved to know he was alright. She tried to file a missing-person's report herself, just as Arthur Parker had attempted to do, but, like Parker, she was told that only family members could do that.

"You need to go down there and file a report," Essie

told Abraham's cousin Cedric, the Shakespeare relative she knew best. "It's been more than six months since anybody's seen that boy."

So on November 9, Cedric went to see Major Joe Halman at the Polk County Sheriff's Office (PCSO) on the same mission he had previously discouraged—to report that Abraham Shakespeare was missing and that he believed his cousin's absence had foul play behind it. Halman, an imposing black man who headed the PCSO's criminal division, was well respected in the department and was trusted in the black community, where law enforcement figures are often looked upon with wariness and trepidation.

Cedric admitted to Major Halman that, months before, he had been paid $5,000 to spread the word that Abraham had gone away on his own accord and to deliver the birthday card and gifts to Elizabeth Walker. Explaining that he and his wife were in financial straits while trying to send their son off to college at the time, Cedric said he'd considered the birthday ruse underhanded but relatively harmless and had thought that it might help ease his Aunt Elizabeth's concerns. He said he had neither confirmed nor denied to his aunt that Abraham had given him the birthday package but understood that she was under that impression. Cedric admitted to having helped foster the idea that Abraham was alive and well but in hiding because he believed it to be true. Now, however, he thought differently.

Halman directed Cedric to the Special Victim's Unit, where investigators homed in on Cedric's chicanery.

"Who gave you the card and that kind of money to do those things?" an investigator asked.

"This woman named Dee Dee Moore," Cedric said.

As they learned more about Cedric's financial ties to Dee Dee, they began to believe that his visit to the sheriff's office was prompted less by concern for his missing cousin than by a hunger to get back at Dee Dee, who lately had been threatening to repossess Cedric's car and possibly even his house, both of which had been provided by Abraham.

Detective Chad McConchie had been with the Polk County Sheriff's Office for more than seven years when the missing-person's report on Abraham Shakespeare hit his desk. On November 10, 2009, the day after Cedric had reported his cousin's curious disappearance, McConchie contacted Dee Dee Moore by cell phone and asked her to come into the sheriff's office for an interview, which she immediately, almost eagerly, agreed to. McConchie asked Detective Chris Lynn to sit in on the interview.

Lynn, the son of a police officer, grew up wanting to be a cop, and once educated and trained in the field, he joined the Polk County Sheriff's Office as a deputy. His imposing stature—six feet five, 250 pounds—disguised a jovial, teddy-bear side that his wife and three small children loved, but on the street, Chris Lynn was known as someone not to mess with.

For the past few years, Lynn had been assigned to the homicide division and had worked hundreds of murder cases with love affairs, drug deals, rape, robbery, kidnapping, and revenge at the core. But he knew that money was also a common motive, and having already learned from McConchie that Dee Dee Moore had taken control of the missing millionaire's assets, Lynn needed to know more. McConchie noted that Abraham's huge winnings appeared to have shriveled to only a million or two by the time he meet Dee Dee, but it was still more money than most people would see in a lifetime. "I've seen people kill for a lot less," Lynn said.

He was soon to learn, as his colleague had, that there was nothing reticent or retiring about Dee Dee Moore. Information cascaded from the woman, as if she could not help but tell every detail, even minutiae. She painted a picture of benign intentions, telling the detectives that she had first met Abraham as the subject of a prospective book project and was excited about the rags-to-riches story, but that she had soon come to realize that Abraham was an unhappy and troubled man—almost cursed by his millions—and that it was only her nature to try to help him. Abraham was itching to leave town to get away from pestering money borrowers, she told the detectives, and he'd even told her he had a fake passport under the name "Rodriguez" so that he could go in and out of the country without detection.

Later that same afternoon, Detectives McConchie and Lynn went to Abraham's home on Redhawk Bend Drive to again meet Dee Dee. She, her teenage son, R. J., and her boyfriend, Shar Krasniqi, were all now living there. They had moved in not long after Abraham was last seen in April.

Dee Dee explained to the detectives that she had

bought the house from Abraham for $655,000 and that he'd been happy to unload the place since he was going away. But she was unable to produce a single document supporting the transaction and, when pressed, switched her story. She hadn't given him the cash outright, she said, but rather had been purchasing his plane and cruise tickets as a means of paying off the house purchase.

"I see," said Lynn, knowing the story didn't add up.

Detective Lynn's subsequent interview of James Valenti, one of the founding partners of the law firm that Abraham had first hired to defend him in Michael Ford's failed 2007 lawsuit over who owned the winning lottery tickets, would give him more reason to believe that Dee Dee's house-sale story was bogus. When Abraham dumped Valenti's firm after months of work on the Ford case and hired Willie Gary to take the case to trial, he left behind an unpaid $20,000 legal bill at the Valenti firm. Attempts to collect the money had been futile, so in 2008, the firm had filed an attorney's lien on Abraham's house. Had the house sale been legitimate, James Valenti advised, the lien would have been discovered during the title search and insurance process and would have had to have been satisfied before a sale could be completed. Valenti told Lynn that it was not until Howard Stitzel contacted him about settling the lien in June of 2009 that he learned the house ownership had changed hands.

The move was also news to Courtney Daniels, Abraham's last known live-in girlfriend. At some time in early 2009—she told detectives she couldn't remember exactly when—Courtney left Lakeland to visit a friend in Saint

Petersburg. Abraham had driven her to the bus station, and that first night away, the two of them talked on the phone for hours. He told her that when she was ready to come back, he would send Judy Haggins to pick her up so she wouldn't have to travel again by bus. But Courtney said she was never able to reach Abraham again, and after a few days of not hearing from him, she spoke with Dee Dee, who told her that Abraham had left town with a new girlfriend, an unidentified woman whom, according to Dee Dee, Abraham had met at a Publix grocery store.

Courtney told detectives that she eventually took a bus back to Lakeland, and Judy Haggins picked her up at the station. But when she arrived at the Lakeland house, Courtney was stunned to learn that Dee Dee, R. J., and Shar had moved in. Not knowing what to think and without any legal claim to the property, Courtney packed her belongings (noticing many of Abraham's belongings still here and there throughout the house) and moved out that day.

Less than a week after Polk County detectives had begun peppering her with questions and digging through her documents, Dee Dee went to see Abraham's ex-girlfriend Sentorria Butler with what she said was something of a peace offering for her troubles with Abraham. Dee Dee wanted to give Jeremiyah's mother a car and the deed to one of the houses she had foreclosed on after taking over Abraham's mortgage loans. All Torrie would have to do in exchange would be to call investigators and assure them that she had recently seen Abraham, Dee Dee explained softly. It would help take some of the heat off Abraham, who was still not paying child support and who had been a no-show at a recent hearing on the matter. Torrie had been at the hearing, where Howard Stitzel told the court that Abraham was unavailable because he was away receiving medical treatment for an unspecified illness or condition. Dee Dee had told her previously that Abraham was suffering from AIDS, but Torrie wasn't sure if that was the condition Stitzel was referring to in court—or if it was even true. All she knew for certain was that Abraham had stiffed her again. Dee Dee acknowledged as much and commiserated with Torrie, telling her she hoped the house and car would help ease the sting of Abraham's slights. Desperate for help in caring for her infant son, Torrie told Dee Dee she would accept the gifts and tell police she had been in touch with Abraham, even though she had not seen his face or heard his voice since April.

Once Dee Dee left, Torrie called detectives, as promised. But instead of repeating Dee Dee's lie, she told them about Dee Dee's car and house offer and her request that Torrie file a false report. The detectives made note of the scheme and added it to the growing pile of evidence suggesting that Abraham Shakespeare might be more than merely missing.

CHAPTER SEVEN

.....

Greg Smith's experience with Dee Dee Moore's crying jag in the Hummer had given him further disturbing insight into the strange character he was dealing with, but he ignored the alarm bells. A couple of days had passed since then, and he still had not received the documents he needed to secure his mother's house, so he felt he had no choice but to continue dealing with the batty woman. How he wished all of this mess would just go away. He flipped open his cell phone and once again dialed Judy Haggins.

"Hey, I need you to set up another meeting with Dee Dee about this paperwork," Greg said. "I want to get this shit over with."

"I'll tell her you need to talk to her," Judy said.

Within minutes, Dee Dee called Greg to say she was

on her way to his barbershop. He winced at the thought of another round of histrionics with the woman.

"Y'all peep out the window," Greg said to the other men in the shop. "This white woman dealing with Abraham, she busted out crying on me the last time. I just need some witnesses that I ain't done nothing to ol' girl."

Shortly thereafter, Dee Dee pulled up in front of the shop, where Greg was waiting, smoking a cigarette.

"Can you take a ride for just a minute?" she asked.

Greg felt his stomach knot up as he moved toward the car. Getting into a car with a big white woman seemed chancy, but he needed those papers and proceeded in hopes that this encounter with the neurotic woman would be his last. He glanced back at the shop window, where three sets of wide eyes were watching. He gave his friends a quick nod and walked around to the passenger door.

"Okay," Greg said. "But I can't go far. I'm working."

Dee Dee steered the big vehicle onto the highway.

"I need a favor," she said. "And you can't tell anybody about it, not even Judy."

"What's wrong with Judy?" Greg asked.

"I don't trust her anymore," Dee Dee said. "You got to promise me you won't tell her any of this."

"All right," Greg said.

"I'll call you later and tell you what I need you to do," she said, rounding the corner and bringing the Hummer to rest at the curb outside Greg's shop. He hopped out, relieved that there had been no histrionics that time, but still without his papers, though now also curious about Dee Dee's "favor" and her unexpected reservations about Judy Haggins.

In the two or three hours between the time he was dropped back off and when he met Dee Dee again that night at a local mall, ostensibly to get the long-promised documents, Greg struggled to keep his mind on his work instead of on that afternoon's brief but cryptic encounter. He found himself so distracted at one point that he sent one of his regular customers to another barber's chair, afraid that his absentmindedness might lead to a mistake with the clippers.

That evening, as he pulled into the mall's parking lot, Greg looked for Dee Dee's black Hummer. When he didn't see it after circling the lot a few times, he dialed Dee Dee.

"Where you at?" he asked.

"Just pull over here by the white truck," she said.

Greg spotted a spanking-new white Chevy 250 diesel truck, and he parked his own Toyota Camry next to it. Dee Dee was behind the wheel, and motioned for Greg to get in.

"What's up, lady?" Greg said, trying to sound nonchalant.

"Greg, these people think I've done something to Abraham," Dee Dee whined. "The cops. They've been to my house; they've searched my house. They've pulled all kinds of computers and records and been through all my stuff."

"Whaaaat?" Greg said. This was the first he'd heard about the police being involved.

"Because Abraham's not around, they think something's up, but nothing's up. I'm just trying to handle his financials while he's away. He doesn't want to come back here right now, he can't come back here right now, and I can't make him come back here. But these detectives keep saying something doesn't add up. I just need to get them off my back until Abraham gets back, 'cause he's on his way home."

"Well, what you want from me?"

"I need you to call this guy. I'll give you $300 to make this call. Don't give your name or nothing. Just call this guy, Dave Wallace and tell him you were down in Miami at a strip club and you saw Abraham Shakespeare and the reason you knew it was him is because he reached in his pocket to get some money and his wallet fell out and you saw his ID."

"Who the hell is Dave Wallace?"

"He's just this guy who's been asking about Abraham. You can tell him that you saw Abraham in Miami and I think that will get these people off my back."

"And you'll pay me $300 and all I got to do is make one phone call?"

"That's all. Three hundred dollars. I got it right here."

Greg did the calculations. Quick call. Anonymous. Spit out a little white lie. Hang up. Collect three bills.

"I can do that," he said.

"Okay, so just go to the gas station right down the road and use the pay phone there. I don't want you to use your phone or my phone. You ought to put a sock or a tissue or something over the phone, make the call then meet me back here and I'll give you the three hundred."

"A'ight. Gimme the number."

Dee Dee handed Greg a scrap of paper with a number scrawled on it, and he returned to his car and headed for the service station a few blocks away. He pulled his car as close to the pay phone as possible, knowing he would want to get away as soon as he finished the call. He cupped his hand over the receiver. It took only two rings for a man to answer.

"This Dave Wallace?" Greg asked, lowering his voice.

"Yeah, this is Dave Wallace. Who is this?"

"It don't matter who this is."

"What's this about?"

"I'm down here in Miami and just want to let you know I saw Abraham Shakespeare in a damn strip club."

"You say you've seen Abraham Shakespeare?"

"Yeah, we was at the same strip club and he reached in his pocket for something and his ID fell out and I saw it was him. Just wanted to tell you that."

"When . . ."

Greg was not about to answer any questions from this guy, whoever he was. He eased the handset into the cradle and hurried to his car, speeding off back toward the parking lot, where Dee Dee waited in the white truck.

"Did you do it?" Dee Dee asked, her eyes wide.

"Yeah, I did it. I called Dave Wallace and told him what you said."

"Do you think he believed it?"

"Shit, I don't know. I wasn't trying to stay on the phone that long. I just told him what you said to say, then hung up."

"Good, good," Dee Dee said, peeling off fifteen twenty-dollar bills. "Maybe that will get them off my back until Abraham comes home." Greg still didn't have his paperwork. But, for the moment, he was content with the crisp bills in his pocket and the fact that he was going home.

Greg didn't know what that last piece of business was really about. He didn't know who the hell Dave Wallace was or why he would be interested in hearing about Abraham. All he knew was that it was the easiest $300 he'd made since his dope-selling days, and for all he knew, no harm, no foul. And apparently it had done the trick, because afterward, he didn't hear from Dee Dee for two weeks. Two blessed weeks, as far as he was concerned. Greg imagined that one day soon, Abraham would pop back into his barbershop, looking better than ever, with stories to tell about his adventures. Greg would make sure his old friend knew about all the trouble his absence had caused—and about the odd dealings with Dee Dee—but he expected that soon enough, they'd all be laughing again, and everything would be back to normal.

Then Dee Dee called to talk about a remodeling job Greg was working on at a friend's house.

"I need another favor," Dee Dee said softly.

"What kind of favor?" Greg asked, unhappy that his reprieve was apparently already coming to an end.

"I need you to make another call."

"What kind of call? Like before?"

"Yeah, like before. And I'll give you $350 this time."

Sheeit, Greg thought. *More easy money. Why not?*

"Okay, swing by the shop and pick me up."

"No, meet me at the parking lot again in two hours."

This time, Greg spotted Dee Dee's big white truck right away. Hopping in, he greeted Dee Dee with a "Whassup?"

"Okay, here's what I need," Dee Dee told him. "I need you to call Abraham's mother and tell her that you're Abraham, and that you're okay but you can't come home because you've gotten into a little trouble at a club for choking a girl in a club and the police are looking for you."

"Say what now?" Greg again felt a knot in his stomach. Making an anonymous call to a stranger and telling him a lie was not such a big deal—especially not for $300—but calling someone's mother and pretending to be her son? That might be going too far.

Dee Dee went on. "And tell her that you'll come to visit her as soon as this blows over, but right now, the cops are looking for you because the girl is pressing charges and you need to wait until it gets straightened out before you come back. You can go and use that pay phone again."

Greg hesitated. *What the hell is going on?*

"Please, Greg. I just need this one last favor," Dee Dee whispered.

Greg knew the stunt was patently deceptive, but he reasoned that it would put a little extra money in his pocket and give an old woman some relief until her son returned home—all in all, a harmless ruse, he told himself.

"I'll make the call," he said, putting his reservations behind him.

"Great. I'm going to pick his mom up and take her to Cracker Barrel where she can't hear your voice good while you're being Abraham because there's a lot of noise in the background."

"Uh-huh."

"When I get there and we get seated, I'm going to text you with a C for *call* and you can do it then." She gave Greg the number to Mrs. Walker's cell phone—a prepaid phone Dee Dee had bought for her.

Greg decided that rather than go to a pay phone, he would use his cell phone to make the call, worried that Dee Dee might be setting him up somehow with the pay-phone locale. Around 6:00 P.M. on December 27, 2009, a text came through from Dee Dee. It was time to make the call.

"Oh, hi, Abraham, it's Dee Dee," Dee Dee exclaimed, intercepting Ms. Walker's phone. "How are you? Yeah, I'm here with your mom, having dinner. Let me let you speak to her."

"Hey, Ma, this Abraham right here," Greg said.

"Hi, baby," Elizabeth Walker said tenderly.

"I just want you to know that I'm okay and I'm gonna see you soon. I'll be home soon."

"Okay, okay."

"And that I love you."

"Okay, okay."

"So, don't worry nothing about me. I'm fine. I'll see you soon."

"Okay. Where you at, baby?"

"I can't hear you too good, Ma, 'cause it's noisy."

"Where are you and when you coming home?"

True to Dee Dee's instructions, Greg ended the call without answering Ms. Walker. It was enough that he was pretending to be her son. He wasn't about to get into a conversation with her.

"You did good," Dee Dee said giddily when she and Greg reconnected in the Dillard's parking lot the next day. "She believed that was Abraham."

"I don't know," Greg said. "Hope so. I did the best I could." He collected his cash from Dee Dee and headed back to a house he had been doing repair work on for a friend before leaving to meet Dee Dee in the lot. As he stopped at a traffic light, three burly white men hopped out the car behind him and swarmed his Camry, one of them tapping on the driver's window.

"Let the windows down; put your hands out of the car!" commanded the man. Another blocked the passenger door.

The three men—Dave Wallace, Chris Lynn, and David Clark, all homicide detectives with the Polk County Sheriff's Office—had been following Greg since he'd left Dee Dee back in the parking lot. Actually, they had been trailing him all morning, having traced the previous evening's phone call to Ms. Walker to his phone and, working with the cell-phone provider, accessing the cell-phone tower's pings to track him to the Dillard's parking lot that morning.

They couldn't believe their luck when Dee Dee had pulled into the lot too, and they'd watched with bated breath as she'd handed Greg several dollar bills. "Some street thug she's using for something," mused Lynn.

"Yep," said Wallace. "Let's see where the ol' boy's going."

As Greg headed back to his work site, the detectives realized they had no police lights on their unmarked car to signal a pullover. So, when Greg stopped for a red light, they bum-rushed his car.

"Look here, buddy," said Clark. "You've got about ten seconds to make a decision that's going to change your life. You can either cooperate with us or we're going to make your life a living hell."

Greg surprised the officers with his calm demeanor. He knew that routine all too well and complied.

"I'll be more than happy to talk to y'all," Greg said pleasantly. "As a matter of fact, I think I know what you want to talk about."

Clark drove Greg's Camry into a nearby parking lot and locked it. With Greg in custody, the detectives sped away, aware that the strange sight might alarm passersby.

"We were these three white guys pulling up on a black dude in the middle of a black neighborhood in Lakeland and speeding away with him," Lynn recalled. "It looked like a kidnapping."

* * *

As he sat in the backseat of the officers' unmarked car, there was no question in Greg's mind that his current circumstances had everything to do with Dee Dee Moore. The woman had been bad news from the start, and right now, he was cursing himself for ever having gotten involved with her.

"We saw you with Dee Dee Moore a little bit ago," said the big man sitting in the backseat with Greg, confirming his suspicions. "How do you know her?"

"She works for this friend of mine and I give her my money to pay him back for a loan," Greg said.

"Did you make phone calls for Dee Dee?"

"Yeah." Greg was going to shoot straight with the cops and make sure they knew that he had no bad intentions whatsoever.

"Did you call Abraham Shakespeare's mother last night?"

"Uh, yeah."

"Did you make a phone call to Dave Wallace a few days ago?"

"Yessir."

"Well, I'm Dave Wallace."

Aw shit! Greg thought. *I called the goddamned police? I'm going to jail for sure now.*

"Look, man, I haven't done nothing," Greg said, plaintively. "I don't know nothing. I apologize for calling your damn phone, man."

"We need to have a little talk with you," said Wallace.

"For what?"

"We're thinking something has happened to Abraham Shakespeare and Dee Dee Moore has something to do with it."

"Aw, man, naw. Look here, that woman paid me to make those phone calls. I didn't mean no harm. And I don't know nothing about something happening to Abraham. He's my friend, man."

"Chill out. We just need to talk to you."

Unnerved by the encounter, Greg knew now that he was not the only one with misgivings about Dee Dee Moore. He wasn't sure why the law was involved, but he knew it could only be something bad, and with his record of felony convictions, Greg was determined to get himself off whatever hook he was on. He was not going back to jail to protect Dee Dee Moore, that was for damn sure.

At the Polk County Sheriff's Office, Greg decided to cut his losses and tell detectives everything he knew about Dee Dee—how Abraham had first introduced them at the beginning of 2009; how he had started making his monthly loan-installment payments to her per Abraham's direction; how those simple transactions had become more complicated and his dealings with her more frequent because of the foreclosure mess; how she had repeatedly insisted that Abraham had left town to avoid trouble and that she was only trying to help him get away from borrowers, debtors, and child-support collectors.

Greg told them that when Dee Dee had hired him to make the anonymous call to Wallace a few days back, claiming to have seen Abraham at a Miami strip club, he hadn't known Wallace was a police officer. And that when he pretended to be Abraham in the call to Mrs. Walker the day before, he thought it would help Abraham's mother relax; no harm intended. He repeatedly apologized for making the bogus phone calls, pleading with the officers to give him a break. "I don't need any trouble," he said.

"Well, then maybe you can help us out," Wallace said.

"Help you out how?" Greg asked.

"We need some help with this. You know there's a missing-person's report out on Shakespeare, right?"

"No, I heard it but I didn't believe that shit."

"Well, we've been checking Dee Dee's business records and she has completely taken over control of Mr. Shakespeare's finances."

"Yeah, that's why I have to deal with her in the first place."

"But, with him missing, it makes the whole thing pretty suspicious. We've been watching Dee Dee for a while now. We've been watching her and tracking her movements. That's how we found you when you met with her in the mall parking lot today."

"Aw, man."

"Right. So we need someone on the inside to help us get to the bottom of this. Maybe nothing has happened to Shakespeare, but it doesn't look good right now.

You're free to go and there's nothing we can do to you, but we do need some help."

Despite the fact that he was in a police-interrogation room once again, Greg felt relieved by Wallace's easy demeanor. But he didn't see how he could help.

"I don't know nothing, man. I can tell you about my own loan and how Dee Dee fucked that up and those two phone calls, but I don't know anything about where Abraham is, why he's gone or when he's coming back. I been trying to reach him myself."

"Right, but we think Dee Dee Moore does know something, and we need someone to help us get information out of her."

"So, what you want me to do?" Greg asked.

"Just keep hanging out with Dee Dee and see if you can get her to talk. Find out what she really knows about Mr. Shakespeare."

"And come back and tell y'all?"

"Right," said Wallace. "And if it gets too interesting, where we need to be involved, we'll wire you up so we can make sure we have an airtight record. All you have to do is get her to talk as much as possible."

"Wire me up? Like on all those detective shows?" Greg asked.

Wallace chuckled. "Something like that."

"And y'all will have my back?"

"We'll be right there."

"Can I think about it? I mean, I ain't really nobody's snitch and I don't want to get caught up in no bullshit."

"You can think it over and get back to us," Wallace said, adding with a smile, "You have my number, right?"

"Man, I threw that number away right after I made that call," Greg said, laughing nervously.

"Yeah, I bet you did. Well, here it is again. And you're not to tell Dee Dee anything about this conversation."

"Maaaaan, I ain't trying to say shit to Dee Dee Moore, you feel me?"

"All right. You get back to me in the next day or two. We'll take you back to your car now."

A long, hot shower washed away the sweat and grime of the day but did nothing to erase the worry that mottled Greg's mind. Nor could the big plate of home cooking or the cold beer he had for dinner that night relax him. All he could think about was the flood of events, the developments and coincidences that had occurred since that day when Shakyboy first brought Dee Dee Moore into his life. He had been leery of her before ever laying eyes on her, and he wished again that he had taken his old friend aside and convinced him that the woman was bad news. Now something was clearly wrong. God forbid that something had actually happened to Abraham, but if it had, Dee Dee was bound to at least know about it, if not had a hand in it. Even if Shakyboy was in trouble, it was time for him to come home and let his friends and family help him.

Wanting to get a grip on just who this Dee Dee Moore really was and what she was up to, Greg decided to call Judy Haggins again. Maybe she could tell him what was going on.

"What's with these crackas saying that white woman has done something to Abraham?" Greg asked as soon as Judy answered the call.

"I don't know," Judy said, nonchalantly.

"Why you even fucking with this? You need to watch out for yourself, girl."

"I'm trying to get me some money out of her now because the simple fact [is], they are coming to get Dee Dee."

Get her for what? Greg wondered. He pressed Judy for details. "Why you say that?" he asked. "Give me some for-instances."

Judy recalled Dee Dee prodding her to report sightings and encounters with Abraham, like the purported visit to Texas. Without her admitting it, Greg now assumed the Texas tale had been a lie. He started to ask Judy outright, but decided it might put her on the defensive and make her feel uncomfortable confiding in him. Besides, he thought, he could read between the lines well enough.

Judy continued recalling Dee Dee's suspicious acts, as if she were putting two and two together for the first time. She told Greg that Dee Dee consistently exaggerated the severity of Abraham's child-support issues, always had a ready excuse for why Abraham wasn't around, and had once asked Judy to keep him from going to the bank to inquire about his accounts.

"When Abraham got ready to go to the bank one day

to see about his money, she called me on the phone frantic," Judy said. "'You've got to stall him, Judy. He can't go to the bank.'" Judy said she'd cooperated with Dee Dee, despite her misgivings, but claimed that she later tried to make it right by urging Abraham to regain control of his assets.

"Abraham used to come to me and say, 'Now you know that white woman got my money, she can do anything to me.' I said, 'Abraham, you can go get your money.'"

"Why don't you go and get his motherfuckin' money, Judy?" Greg asked, agitated by Judy's passivity. "Don't you have power of attorney? He did that for a reason. Just go move his fucking money and put it where it's supposed to be. 'Cause if that ho did something to Abraham, I'm gone sink her ass. I'm telling you that cracka don't like you, hear? I'm looking out for you."

Seemingly put at ease by Greg's protectiveness, Judy confessed that Dee Dee's conflicting accounts of what had happened to Abraham and her desperate recruitment of people to tell and spread lies and alibis had her thinking that maybe Dee Dee *had* done something to Abraham after all.

Greg advised Judy to be extra careful in dealing with Dee Dee. In his opinion, the big blonde was under so much pressure that she might throw anyone under the bus, including her sidekick. Dee Dee had already told him that she didn't trust Judy anymore. If nothing else, Dee Dee might try to blame any financial shenanigans on her, considering Judy's power of attorney.

"Dee Dee forgot she need to be on my team," Judy agreed. "I'm the one she told all this to. Once these people start putting all this stuff together, they'll build a case against her. I said, 'Why does Abraham got me as power of attorney and he won't talk to me?' That don't look right."

"Well, you just try to stay away from that bitch," Greg cautioned. "And don't ever say anything about you and me talking, you hear?"

"No problem," Judy said.

Having absorbed Judy Haggins's misgivings on top of his own, Greg dragged himself up from the sofa and dialed Dave Wallace's number. Though exhausted by all of the back-and-forth with Dee Dee and Judy, all of his instincts were firing now. Everything in him told him that Dee Dee was a dirty player who had tricked Abraham out of his money, had probably gotten rid of him somehow, and had manipulated weak-minded, desperate people into helping her cover up what she had done.

"This Greg Smith, right here. The dude you talked to about Abraham Shakespeare," Greg said.

"Right. I know who you are," Wallace responded.

"Abraham is dead, Detective Wallace."

"How do you know?"

"It's just a gut feeling." He had no better explanation than that.

"Yeah, we've been feeling that way for a while now."

"Well, I been thinking about this and working it over in my mind."

"Yeah."

"I been putting two and two together and now the whole picture is coming into focus, you know what I'm saying?"

"Right. Same with us, Greg."

"Yeah, but I just wasn't seeing it until now. It was strange and I had some suspicions, but I really believed that Abraham had just fucked up somewhere, but was all right and would be back."

"And now you've come to a different conclusion?"

"Now I *know* something ain't right."

"That's what we've been saying."

"You know, this is new to me, but Abraham was my friend, man, and he don't deserve anything bad happening to him. Dude has been through enough in his life. He just tried to help folks out when he got that money. It hurts my heart that somebody would hurt him."

"Right."

"So, I just want to let you know that I'm in. Whatever I got to do, I'm all in."

CHAPTER EIGHT

•••••

Dave Wallace had wanted to be a cop for as long as he could remember. Maybe it was because of his dad, a former police officer in Pompano Beach, Florida, who Dave had looked up to and who introduced him, however casually, to the world of law enforcement. Because of his dad's work, Dave grew up around cops and liked their uniforms, their swagger, what they stood for.

After college and law enforcement training, Wallace found a home for his calling at the Polk County Sheriff's Office (PCSO) in 1996. Deputy Wallace's intelligence, methodical style, and good-naturedness was a good fit for the busy PCSO, charged with keeping the peace—or restoring it—among more than 600,000 souls of assorted temperament and circumstance scattered over two thousand square miles of central Florida. For cops like Wallace who enjoyed variety and action, Polk County was a pretty good place to be, even after his first sheriff left and die-hard right-winger Grady Judd was elected in 2004, bringing with him a flamboyant, brash, unflinching style that few locals had ever seen at the helm of their law enforcement. Judd had vowed to crack down hard on drug crimes in the county, and, assigned to the Narcotics Unit, Dave Wallace soon had a full plate of cases involving shady and often violent users, manufacturers, and dealers.

It wasn't long after Abraham Shakespeare's cousin Cedric Edom showed up at the sheriff's office on that November day in 2009 to file a missing person's report that Wallace, by now a homicide detective, was assigned to the case. The missing-person's team had sniffed around a bit at first, mainly at the house Dee Dee Moore had taken over from Abraham, and found the circumstances fishy enough to move the case directly over to the homicide division. There was more to it than a mere disappearing act, they quickly surmised.

Wallace was one of four detectives assigned to Polk County's Cold Case Unit, a band of seasoned investigators always on the lookout for new leads and evidence in unresolved murder cases. Because of their experience and expertise in uncovering obscurities and fishing out arcane leads, the Cold Case guys were often called upon to handle active cases that were especially complicated and troublesome, as the Shakespeare case was shaping up to be.

Wallace had just wrapped up the nettlesome case of twenty-one-year-old Davion Parsons, who'd skipped town and fled to his native Jamaica with multiple charges of first-degree murder in Polk County hanging over his head. Wallace was one of several detectives who tracked Parsons down, setting off a yearlong extradition battle that had finally ended with Parsons's return to Polk County in October 2009.

It was shortly thereafter that the missing-person's guys notified the homicide team that the Abraham Shakespeare case begged their attention, so by early November 2009, Wallace and fellow detective David Clark began lining up witnesses to interview as Detective Chris Lynn continued combing through Abraham's bank records and other financial documents.

Lynn's forays into the multilayered world of Dee Dee Moore's finances raised red flags galore, especially a particular Bank of America account under the name of Abraham Shakespeare, LLC. In his official report, Lynn noted something curious about activity on the account following a deposit of $1,095,000 the first week of February 2009.

"From February 11th through 17th, not one deposit, withdrawal or transfer affects the account," Lynn wrote in his report. "However, on February 18th, in excess of $700,000 leaves via withdrawals in the form of cashier's checks." As Lynn noted, all of the checks were made payable to Dee Dee's company, except for one to the U.S. Internal Revenue Service. But Lynn reported that even the check to the IRS was suspicious because Dee Dee had signed it "with a note under the endorsement stating 'not needed for intended purpose' and subsequently deposited into the Bank of America business account of American Medical Professionals."

In one week, Lynn wrote, "The seed money of the account which began in excess of one million dollars had been depleted to approximately $50,000 remaining." Further, Dee Dee's was the only authorized signatory on the account bearing Abraham's name.

Until Cedric Edom filed the missing-person's report, Wallace and Clark—like most people outside of Abraham's circle of friends and haunts—only knew of Abraham Shakespeare from what they had seen in the news about his lottery win. It was no surprise that the man had become exceedingly popular in Lakeland, and they knew there would be plenty of people to talk to about the local celebrity. Lynn had already interviewed Dee Dee Moore twice—once at the sheriff's office and again at the house on Redhawk Bend Drive—when Wallace and Clark got their first face-to-face with the woman with the curious ties to the missing multimillionaire.

Like Wallace, Clark had worked in narcotics earlier in his career, chasing down drug dealers and suppliers—gritty, dangerous work that imbued the kind of street smarts that made the men hard to fool and adept at reading between the lines. He'd been working as an emergency medical technician in his native Polk County in the mid-1990s when the prospect of going into law enforcement first presented itself. A deputy had been shot during a standoff in Polk County, and it had taken longer than usual for an ambulance to get to him because gunfire was still erupting in the area. From then on, the sheriff decided, his SWAT team would include EMTs so that no other officer wounded in the line of duty would have to wait for emergency treatment on an active crime scene. David Clark was one of the first to take the new job.

The experience was an awakening. Clark realized that he loved the action, the unpredictability, the authority, the camaraderie, and the sense of service that came with being a cop. He enrolled in a law enforcement academy and, upon graduation, went to work for the police department in Winter Haven, a sedate Polk County community famous for its chains of lakes and an eighty-year stretch as the spring-training home of top Major League Baseball teams like the Philadelphia Phillies, the Boston Red Sox, and the Cleveland Indians.

Genial and outgoing, Clark prided himself on being fair, even to some of the subjects he was trying to nail. When he helped negotiate lesser charges for a local criminal who Clark believed deserved a second chance, the fellow returned the favor by offering to help Clark nab the man who had killed a twenty-two-year-old named Carlton Potts, one of Polk County's most notorious drug dealers, during a robbery in late 2006.

With a willing and able informant in tow, Clark was appointed to a federal task force charged with solving the Potts murder, which, in turn, put him in regular contact with officers from Polk County, the scene of the crime. After Jermaine Michael Jillian was arrested for breaking into "The Carter"—the nickname for the drug house where the slaying occurred—and fatally shooting Potts, Polk County Sheriff's Office offered Clark a job in its homicide division. That was 2007. He and Wallace became partners and all but instant best friends, with Clark often playing "good cop" to Wallace's "bad cop," roles they used with Dee Dee Moore.

She was her usual voluble self in that first meeting with Wallace and Clark. Having already interviewed Dee Dee twice himself, Lynn was nearly as interested in his colleagues' reaction to her as he was to anything Dee Dee had to say. As she chatted away about her relationship with Abraham, his disappearance, and how much she had tried to help him, Lynn could see the blood rushing to Wallace's face.

"You know what I think, Dee Dee?" Wallace finally said. "I think Abraham Shakespeare is dead and I think you know he's dead."

"I absolutely do not," Dee Dee said, huffily. "I told you he wanted to get away from all these people who are bothering him all the time and his boy's mother and all of these folks asking for money and owing him money."

Wallace pressed on, showing no sympathy for Dee Dee as she whimpered through a litany of kindnesses she had showered upon Abraham.

"Now I've got all this trouble on me when all I was trying to do is help the man," she cried.

As Wallace shut down, Clark, flush with feigned compassion, pulled his chair closer to Dee Dee and leaned in.

"Dee Dee, I don't mind telling you that I want to believe you," he said softly. "Like you said, all you have been trying to do is help Abraham. You shouldn't have to go through this."

Dee Dee wept quietly, wrapping her arms around herself and nodding.

"But you're going to have to give us something to go on if we're going to find Abraham and get you out of this," Clark continued. He could tell she wanted the detectives to like her and feel sorry for her. If Wallace's hard-assed approach had shaken her up, maybe a sympathetic touch would make her cave.

"But I don't know nothing more than what I told you," Dee Dee sniveled. "All I know is that Abraham told me he couldn't take it no more and had to get away and he said, 'You handle all the business, I got to go' and all I've been trying to do is keep things in order until he gets back. And I'm sure he's going to come back before too much longer because he told his mama he was coming back soon. And all I know is that I just wanted to help the man. And . . ."

"That's enough for now," Wallace said, interrupting the pity party.

"You're free to go. We'll be in touch."

He'd had all the lies he could take in one sitting.

As the detectives discovered soon enough, they were far from the only ones with qualms about Dee Dee Moore. Many people in Lakeland had plenty to say about the tall white woman who had been accompanying Abraham almost everywhere he went at the beginning of the year, portraying herself as a guardian angel come to help when the pressure of managing so much money had gotten to be too much for the man. Rumors swirled around Lakeland's black community that Abraham was on the lam from borrowers, from child-support enforcement, from police, from drug dealers. People heard he was on vacation in the Caribbean or making the round of gentlemen's clubs in Miami. There was word that he had moved to Orlando with a new girlfriend. One rumor even had it that Abraham was in the final throes of AIDS and living out his last days in a nursing home. Longtime friend Glenda McRay told Wallace and Clark she had heard Abraham died in a Tampa hospital.

Most of the rumors could be traced, at some point, to Dee Dee Moore, who either spread the falsehoods herself, or urged—or paid—someone else to do so. Witness after witness, whether friend, borrower, or family member, expressed suspicion that Dee Dee's appearance on the scene and Abraham's disappearance were not coincidences. It was not so much what they knew but what their guts told them: Dee Dee Moore was up to no good.

Eddie Dixon, another of Abraham's old friends, told authorities that Dee Dee "popped out of nowhere," and that once she'd entered the picture, Abraham stopped hanging out with him at the Super Choice store. "I feel like this woman knows where he is," Dixon said, reflecting the consensus within Abraham's circle. Tony Edom, Cedric's younger brother, told detectives his cousin would not leave the area without telling someone in the family where he was going and without making contact for months. Every relative said something similar.

When Dee Dee Moore again presented herself to the Polk County Sheriff's Office at the request of investigators in mid-November, Wallace braced himself for more of her invariable barrage of excuses, alibis, theories, and self-pity. Far from a reluctant interviewee, Dee Dee seemed to love the sound of her own voice. One simple question could open the floodgates. Her repetitive and tangled monologues always pointed the detectives in myriad directions and were so rife with inconsistencies that the sessions often added only another layer of confusion to an already overladen pile. When detectives confronted her about the discrepancies between what she claimed and what they found to be true, Dee Dee would change her story yet again, always portraying herself as a guileless do-gooder. But Wallace and Clark had no doubt she was hiding something, and within days of taking the case, they began to believe that something might be Abraham Shakespeare's dead body.

Armed with search warrants and subpoenas, the detectives spent the Thanksgiving holiday rummaging through Dee Dee's computer files and land, bank, property, and business records. As they gathered the puzzle pieces, the detectives' hunch that Abraham Shakespeare was not only missing, but dead grew into all but a certainty. Still, Dee Dee continued to insist that her old patron was on the run and that no one wanted him to come back more than she, whose family, health, and business were all suffering under the thickening clouds of suspicion.

"Why did he leave, Dee Dee?" Wallace had asked her in one interview.

"Because he wanted to pretend that he was dying of AIDS so that he doesn't have to pay child support. And people won't look for him if he's dying of AIDS."

Wallace had heard the AIDS rumor, but investigators had found nothing to substantiate it. Now he knew why. Even Dee Dee said it was all a pretense to throw people off his trail.

And there was something else that had her friend on the run, she added in one of her patented, singsong whispers, as if imparting a secret to cohorts. "It's a videotape of him having sex with a fourteen-year-old girl." She said Abraham was afraid that he would draw a charge if the tape ever fell into police hands. Then she broke down.

"My family's being affected; my mom's got heart problems. She's over at my house right now cleaning for Thanksgiving. My own parents were scared to come to my house for Thanksgiving," she sobbed.

Wallace's fellow investigator Clark played the sympathy card, assuring Dee Dee that he understood her frustration and urging her to do all she could to persuade Abraham to return—a ploy that was so effective that, in a subsequent interview, Dee Dee would make a sexual proposition to Clark, offering to get a hotel room so that the two of them could have a good time.

Wallace, once more playing the proverbial bad cop to Clark's good cop, was the hard-ass.

"I honestly can't look at you and believe a word that's coming out of your mouth," he told the sobbing woman.

Considering all possibilities, detectives tracked down Michael Ford, Abraham's old trucking partner, just in case he still carried a grudge over losing his lawsuit and had exacted some revenge. Shortly after the trial ended, in mid-fall 2007, Michael Ford said in his telephone interview, he moved to Carrollton, Georgia, where he got a job as an over-the-road truck driver for FedEx. Since then, he had only been back to central Florida two or three times, always going straight to the company terminal to unload, then hitch another trailer and drive back to Georgia. He hadn't seen Abraham since the day they walked out of court in 2007. And he had no idea where he was. Ford was one of several potential suspects ruled out early in the probe.

It was late December 2009 when Dave Wallace received the anonymous phone call from a man claiming to have seen Abraham Shakespeare in a Miami strip club, but there was nowhere to go with it. *Probably just a crank call*, he'd thought. After all, newspapers and television news had picked up on the missing-person's report, thanks to Abraham's celebrity, so the caller was probably a nobody longing for a cheap thrill. The detective had seen it happen before.

Back in 1997, when cops were looking for killer Andrew Cunanan, whose murderous rampage had left fashion designer Gianni Versace dead on his mansion steps in Miami, loads of people had called into the Polk County Sheriff's Office—two hundred miles from Miami—swearing that they had just seen the fugitive killer nearby. Wallace imagined the strange call about an Abraham Shakespeare sighting was the same thing: someone just looking for attention, or maybe a reward. After Abraham had failed to resurface for Thanksgiving, which his family said was one of his favorite holidays, Sheriff Judd had authorized the posting of a $5,000 reward for information leading to the missing man's whereabouts. Predictably, the switchboard lit up with callers claiming to know where Abraham Shakespeare was, but most claims were outlandish, and even the plausible ones had failed to pan out.

But the detective had reacted differently to the phone call Elizabeth Walker received two days after Christmas as she and Dee Dee sat at a local Cracker Barrel restaurant having dinner. He and his team watched in wonder the next day, as Dee Dee approached a slender black man in a Camry and handed him a wad of cash. They knew they were on to something.

Now detectives knew what that call was about, and they knew the guy who had placed it. And here he was, standing among the lawmen as a teammate of sorts. Greg Smith was now on board to help the officers get to the bottom of Dee Dee's involvement with Abraham and what role she might have had in his disappearance.

They'd needed someone who could gain Dee Dee's confidence, and Greg seemed to be just what the doctor ordered. The detectives would have to set boundaries, of course—they wanted to be sure Greg didn't do or say anything that amounted to entrapment, for example—and make sure he stayed on the up-and-up with them, but there were safeguards for that. For one thing, before and after every planned rendezvous between Dee Dee and Greg, deputies would pat down their informant and search his car to make sure there was nothing there to jeopardize the case, threaten the peace, or blow Greg's cover and credibility.

Wallace and Clark were accustomed to working with CIs—confidential informants—from their days in the narcotics division, where officers count on that kind of insider, undercover assistance to get the goods on shady suppliers and dealers. Typically, homicide cases—where the challenge lies in collecting suspects, witnesses, and evidence—do not make much use of CIs. Then again, this was no typical murder case. This was a much more muddled and complex situation. Though every instinct told them otherwise, they couldn't even be 100 percent certain that it *was* a murder case. First and foremost, where on earth Abraham Shakespeare might be, alive or dead, was still anyone's guess. The lawmen needed a break. They needed someone who could get inside Dee Dee's head—a bullshit artist in his own right—a wily, quick-thinking, streetwise tough who could cut through the pile of manure Dee Dee had built. Someone like Greg Smith.

Not everyone in the Polk County Sheriff's Office was on board with the investigators' theory that Dee Dee had manipulated Abraham and had a hand in his disappearance. Nor did they all approve of the detectives' tactics. Cynics abounded. As the main investigators on the case, Wallace, Clark, and Lynn were frequently confronted by half-joking colleagues who maintained that Abraham's disappearance and Dee Dee's deceptions were all just crazy coincidences they were reading too much into. After all, it wasn't as if Abraham's absence was inconceivable. Wealth aside, he had never been a pillar or mainstay of the community; he was known to be a rolling stone. It wasn't so surprising that he might want to get away from all of the panhandling and perhaps have a little fun in the meantime, they argued. And wasn't he being hounded over child support for his second son? The investigators' endless round of interviews, search warrants, document dumps, and surveillance was a waste of time and resources, said the critics. And the idea of bringing on Greg Smith, an ex-con, was just ratcheting up the drama and risk of failure unnecessarily.

Despite their colleagues' doubts, however, Wallace and his team knew they could not ignore the mounting evidence that Dee Dee Moore had been helping herself to Abraham's money and property while unable to stick to one story, let alone several, as to why the man was not around to oversee those matters himself, or where he might be, or when he would return to Lakeland. Though Wallace did not yet know definitively what had happened to Abraham, all of his seasoned instincts told him that the man was gone for good, and that even if Dee Dee didn't have a major role in Abraham's disappearance, she at least knew who did. Wallace also knew that there was a good possibility that the same streetwise qualities that made Greg Smith seem suspicious to other officers could actually be helpful in breaking the case. It would take a special type of personality to beat Dee Dee Moore at her own game—and Wallace had faith that Greg Smith was that guy.

With the investigation in full swing by early December 2009, unbeknownst to Greg Smith at the time, Dee Dee went on the offensive. Rather than shrink from the suspicion encircling her, she continually initiated contact with Polk County detectives to answer questions they had not even asked and offer up new information about Abraham's status, now often insinuating that his absence had something to do with unnamed drug dealers.

When her outreach to the investigators failed to ward them off, Dee Dee reached out to local news-media outlets to get her side of the story out. She even shared a videotape she had made back in early April, showing Abraham standing in a bedroom, pointing a remote control at a television monitor with split-screen images from home-security cameras. As he surfed through the images, Dee Dee—never seen on camera—plied him with questions.

"Do you get tired of people asking you for money all the time, Abe?" she asked. "Give me your opinion on it."

"I been tired," Abraham said with a scowl. "A year ago."

"You just ready to start living your life, huh?"

"They don't take no for an answer, so I just let 'em keep on and keep on asking."

"Um hmm. So where you wanna go to?"

"It don't matter to me. I'm not a picky person."

"California? You want a foreign country? Cozumel?"

Abraham seemed mildly annoyed by the interview.

"Well, how do you like . . ." Dee Dee started. "Are you gonna miss your home?"

"Yep, I miss it," said Abraham. "But life goes on."

Dee Dee told journalists she made the tape because Abraham was preparing to take off, and she had been anticipating questions like the ones she was now getting about his plans and whereabouts.

"He planned on running," Dee Dee told Merissa Green, a reporter for the *Ledger* newspaper in Lakeland, during a three-hour interview she gave in early December. "He planned on not coming back. He intentionally did not want to be found. He didn't care what it took."

Presenting herself as an undeserving target of law enforcement's suspicions, Dee Dee told the reporter that detectives had rifled through her papers and computers. "Then, the other day, [the police] took it over the top," she complained. "I had my stuff blue-lighted to look for blood. It wasn't supposed to end up like this." Like the *Ledger*, other news outlets received offers for interviews from the distraught woman. On several occasions, Dee Dee promised face-to-face interviews with Abraham himself but never delivered. "I want these idiots, these drug heads and these cokeheads to know that I've sold everything," Dee Dee told the *Ledger*. "Abraham sold me his mess to get a better life and I practically gave it away to get mine back."

Meanwhile, the book idea she had originally used to nab an introduction to Abraham was still in play. "I don't feel like I lost anything because the book is going to be phenomenal," she told the *Ledger*. "The book is priceless."

Dee Dee had been working other angles, too. A week after the newspaper article appeared, on December 5, Detectives Wallace, Clark, and Lynn travelled to Perry, Florida, a good two-hundred miles northwest of Lakeland, to speak with Florestine Powell, Abraham's forty-nine-year-old sister. A local police officer accompanied them to Florestine's home.

Earlier in the day, Dee Dee had called Clark to tell him that Florestine had some valuable information to share. She said she had called Abraham's older sister to see how she was doing in light of the recent media coverage and to ask if she had heard from her brother. According to Dee Dee, an anonymous person had recently called Florestine claiming to be calling for Abraham and informing her that her brother was on his way to see her.

Now, face-to-face with Florestine, detectives told her what Dee Dee had said. She told them the anonymous call struck her as peculiar both in circumstance and content. It would have been unlike Abraham to pay her a visit. He had only been to Perry on two occasions: once on his way to Tallahassee to collect his lottery check and again when their older sister had died. Moreover, said

Florestine, she had just gotten an unexpected call from a reporter with the *St. Petersburg Times*. According to the message left on Florestine's voice mail, the journalist wanted to interview her. She didn't return his call because she did not want to deal with the news media and had expressly told Dee Dee so, forbidding her brother's emissary from sharing her phone number with anyone, she said. Florestine said she thought it was all too much of a coincidence. The detectives knew it was.

As Dave Wallace saw it, Dee Dee's decision to go on the offensive was all part of a guilty woman's attempt to cover up something dastardly. Yet her efforts to divert attention from herself had achieved the opposite effect. The detectives had seen it more times than they could count: a guilty person who won't shut up and only digs a deeper hole of incrimination.

"If she would have come in and said, 'Look, I don't know where Abraham is. Here's the deal: he gave me his phone, but I don't know anything else,' it might have stopped there." But the more Dee Dee talked, the guiltier she looked, he said, adding, "She thinks she's smarter than everyone else."

CHAPTER NINE

·····

Greg Smith puffed nervously on his menthol cigarette as the detectives fiddled with his T-shirt on a deserted roadside. The peanut-sized microphone had to be positioned just so. It needed to be centered on his chest in order to pick up both speakers' voices. Luckily, it was January so Greg's extra layers of clothing would not raise Dee Dee's suspicions. Detectives Dave Wallace and David Clark worked together to clip the mike onto Greg's undershirt, running the thin cord around to his waistband, and curling it around to his back, where the transmitter was situated. Greg pulled his shirt over the contraption and walked around, bending and twisting occasionally to make sure it didn't come loose.

"Y'all gonna be monitoring this the whole time, right?" he asked.

"Every word," Wallace said.

"And there won't be any beeping or nothing like that?"

"Absolutely not. No one will know you're wired unless you tell them."

"Well, trust that I won't be telling nobody, you feel me?"

Greg couldn't believe he was doing this, helping the police. His dealings with the law had always been from the other side. He had studiously avoided men and women with badges and guns, people who had the authority to take his freedom away. He'd been cooperative enough whenever he was stopped, frisked, arrested, or questioned, but he had never tried to make it especially easy for them to do their job. Truth be told, Greg had always kind of enjoyed the cat-and-mouse game, the catch-me-if-you-can challenge of outwitting the po-po. He damn sure had never worked with them to bring someone else down. He'd adhered to the I-ain't-no-snitch code of the streets.

But this was different. This was no ordinary, run-of-the-mill investigation with some petty drug charge at stake. This was serious—this was life or death. More than that, this was about finding Abraham, an old friend who had suffered enough hard knocks in life and who had barely even been able to enjoy his own good fortune before getting hassled to pieces by money grubbers, sued by his own former coworker, and likely experienced even worse at the hands of his so-called friend and ersatz money manager, Dee Dee Moore. Greg kept reminding himself that Abraham hadn't done anything but help people—total strangers sometimes—after he won the lottery, and he'd been the least generous with himself. Shakyboy was no saint, and he hadn't always done the right thing, but he was a good dude who wouldn't hurt anyone. So Greg had decided that if someone had done him wrong—physically, financially, or otherwise—he owed it to his buddy not to let that person get away with it.

"Just try to be sure you all are in as quiet a place as possible," the detective said as Greg prepared to leave for his meeting with Dee Dee. "We don't want to lose anything to a bunch of static or background noise."

"We're gonna be in my car," Greg said. "I already thought about that."

He exchanged handshakes and nods with the officers, who had already checked out his car to ensure that there were no weapons, contraband, or anything that might interfere with the transmission or compromise the integrity of the operation. They told Greg they would be parked nearby in an unmarked car.

"So if this bitch gets crazy or something . . ." Greg began.

"We're right there," Wallace assured him.

"Okay, then," Greg said. "Let's do this thing."

Greg immediately spotted Dee Dee in the parking lot at Denny's in Plant City and motioned her over to his car.

"Get in," he said. "We can't talk in your car no more; it might be hot. They might be trailing you."

"How are you?" Dee Dee said, plopping into the Camry's front passenger seat. "You been okay?"

"I been good," Greg said. "Just glad I could make it

this time 'cause my wife needed the car to get to her class, but it all worked out. So, how you been?"

"Greg, I tell you, I'm trying to be calm about all this, but these cops keep bugging me with all these search warrants and questions. And everybody's saying I ripped Abraham off and . . ."

"Fuck them. They don't know what the fuck they're talking about."

"But, the cops . . ."

"Hey, I'm gonna help you get out of this shit. You ain't done nothing; I know that. Abraham just needs to show up. But until he comes back, I'm gonna help you."

Just then, Dee Dee lunged for Greg, groping his arms and chest. Fortuitously, Greg had earlier decided to move the microphone to the left, away from the person in the passenger seat. Still, Dee Dee's frantic fingers came perilously close to finding the small device beneath his shirt.

In those mere seconds, Greg felt panic swelling in his head. *What the hell am I gonna do now?* he thought. *I'm busted.*

"Hey, hey!" Greg shouted. "What the fuck you doing? You don't know me to put your hands all over me!"

Frightened by the outburst, Dee Dee immediately recoiled.

"What the hell? Are you the police or some shit?" Greg demanded. "You trying to set me up or some shit?"

"No, I . . ."

"Get the fuck out of my car!"

"No, Greg, I just . . ."

"Get your motherfucking ass out my car, right now!"

"I'm sorry," she said, sobbing as she collapsed against the backrest. "I just don't know who to trust and I just . . ."

"You just almost fucked up the only friend you got!" Greg said, angrily. "I should have knocked your mother-fucking ass out. Putting your hands all on me like that."

"I am soooo sorry, Greg," Dee Dee sobbed. "You are so nice. I don't know why you're being so nice to me. I see why Abraham says you're a good friend. You are, Greg, and I'm sorry."

"Well, you can't come at me like that," Greg said, adjusting his shirt. "I'm a black man dealing with a white woman in Polk County, Florida. Grady Judd is the sheriff. I ain't trying to go to jail. So don't get me to the point where I can't trust you."

Greg's reaction seemed to reassure Dee Dee, who began to regale him with compliments and thanks for this loyalty, first to Abraham and now to her. She hadn't been able to trust anyone for a long time, she said. The police were making her nuts, and their persistence had upended her life. As calm now as she had been seemingly hysterical only moments before, Dee Dee explained that Abraham had left her holding the bag, having to clean up all of his messes and take the heat for his decision to bolt.

"And the thanks I get is cops calling me all the time and me spending money to pay Abraham's tax bills and all this shit around town about 'where is Abraham' and 'what happened to Abraham' and stuff," she whined.

"Well, we gonna get this straightened out and closed down," Greg said, a cigarette dangling from his mouth. He took a drag, then took a swig from his half-gone Red Bull.

"You don't know how much it means to me that you're going to help me," Dee Dee said sweetly. "I just want to thank you for believing in me and being on my side."

"I'm here for you, baby," Greg said, charmingly. "You just have to stay calm and do what you got to do."

"Okay," Dee Dee said, fiddling with her purse. "Stay calm and do what I got to do. Right. And we'll figure this out."

"We'll figure it out. We in this together, baby."

"Okay. So, I'm gonna go now. I'll talk to you later, okay."

"You got my number."

"And, thank you, Greg. You forgive me, right?"

"It's all good, babe. You just calm yourself down. We'll get through this."

Greg watched as Dee Dee got out of his car, sashayed to her own car, and pulled away. He waited until she'd turned off onto the road before leaving his spot and driving down the road a couple of miles before pulling over. He took a deep breath, lit another cigarette, and lowered his chin to speak directly into the microphone still taped to his chest.

"Wallace, I hope y'all heard all that," he said. "That shit was close, man. I thought for a minute there the jig was up."

Greg went home, still shaken by the microphone fiasco. Although detectives assured him that he had handled things smartly, Greg shuddered to think that, had he not moved the mike on a whim, Dee Dee surely would have discovered it when she'd grabbed him, and the whole plan could have been ruined. At the same time, he was more determined than ever to find out what Dee Dee was up to. He was now certain that the detectives were right; something funny was going on with her endless, varying excuses about Abraham's absence. Whether it was just a money scam or something more sinister didn't matter now. Greg was determined to get to the bottom of it and didn't want to blow his opportunity to help nail Dee Dee Moore. But he didn't like close calls either, and the manhandling in the car had almost exposed him.

A few days later, Greg was mindlessly scrolling through the TV channels, hoping to land on something that would distract him from the worry swimming through his head. As he passed the Discovery Channel, Greg bolted upright, suddenly remembering a "How It's Made" episode about manufacturing soft-drink cans he'd seen years earlier. Greg recalled watching how the body of the soda canister was made first, then filled with liquid. The top—the lid with the pull tab—was then welded onto the can. Because of his sideline work as a carpenter and handyman, Greg knew that meant there had to be a seam where the two pieces met, and that if top and bottom had been put together, they could also be taken apart.

Excited by the memory, Greg raced to the kitchen and plucked an empty Red Bull can from the trash. He ran to his workshop and retrieved a sheet of sandpaper and began rubbing the rim of the can. The process was slow and painstaking; Greg was getting nowhere. So, he put the can on his grinding wheel and slowly abraded it until a hint of a seam appeared. As if about to open a long-lost treasure, Greg sat the can down and stood back to behold it for a moment. He closed his eyes, swallowed hard, and rubbed his hands together in anticipation. He gingerly lifted it from the worktable and flicked his thumb at the faint seam. The top disk popped off immediately.

Greg ran to a desk drawer, tossing aside envelopes and rubber bands until he found his wife's small digital tape recorder. He set it inside the dismantled can and reapplied the top disk. It was a perfect fit. To keep the recorder from rattling around in the canister, Greg inserted some Styrofoam, creating a snug environment for the device. He turned the recorder on, replaced it in the can and gave it a test. On playback, every word came through intelligibly.

Greg rehearsed the scenario in his mind. He would keep the can in a cup holder in his car's console, and tell Dee Dee that since her cars were under surveillance, all future meetings would have to take place in his car. That way, he could capture his and Dee Dee's conversations without facing the risk of detection from wearing a wire. And since he always had a Red Bull energy drink in hand, Dee Dee would think nothing of it.

"Yeah, boy," Greg said with a sigh of relief. He set his homemade creation on the coffee table and stared at it, self-satisfied and proud of his ingenuity. "Where there's a will, there's a way." He couldn't wait to tell Wallace and Clark about it. But, for now, finally feeling a little less anxious, Greg toppled off to sleep.

* * *

"What in the hell. . . ?" Wallace asked, befuddled by Greg's new invention. The informant had arrived at the rendezvous point with the jerry-rigged device in hand.

"That's where the tape recorder is," Greg explained.

"Inside that Red Bull can?"

"Yep. I ground it down so the top comes off and the recorder fits right down in there."

"Does it work? Can you actually hear things?"

"Yep."

"I mean, clearly?"

"Let's see." Greg removed the can top and pulled the recorder from its nest and pressed a button.

"'Does it work? Can you actually hear things?'" came a voice from the recorder. "'Yep.' 'I mean, clearly?' 'Let's see.'"

"I'll be damned," said Wallace. "Pretty damn cool, man, pretty damn cool."

"Thought y'all might like it," Greg said, smugly. "I just knew we had to do something different 'cause that wire shit was not gonna work. I can't get all huffy and tell the bitch to get out of the car and are you the police trying to set me up and all that shit every time."

"You don't want to be felt up by Dee Dee Moore, man?" Clark asked sarcastically. "What's wrong with you?"

"Man, I don't want that big bitch to touch me ever again," Greg insisted.

The men laughed heartily, enjoying a rare moment of levity in the midst of such serious business.

"Well, alright then," said Wallace. "We'll give it a try. I tell you, that beats all. But, hey man, good thinking."

"Thanks," said Greg. "I promise you this is going to work. She won't have any idea."

"Just try to get her to talk as much as you can," Wallace told Greg, as he prepared to leave. "Try to get her to do most of the talking."

"Gotcha," said Greg.

"Have you heard from her?"

"Not yet, but I will. And I'll be ready now."

"Just give us the heads-up . . ."

"Right."

"So we can get into position."

As Greg moved toward his car, Wallace and Clark slapped his back and shook his hand.

"You'll be using our tape recorders from now on," Clark said.

"Make sure they're real little ones like mine," Greg said. "Y'all laughing but this shit gonna work great."

CHAPTER TEN

......

Florida's subtropical climate commonly produces readings in the seventies or eighties even during the winter months. So for natives and longtime residents, forty- or fifty-degree weather means bringing out the heavy coats, scarves, and gloves. The new year of 2010 had brought with it some unusually cold days, and January 20 was one of them. Greg had planned to spend the chilly day indoors, perhaps tooling around in his workshop or running errands with his wife, but one of Dee Dee's frantic we-have-to-meet calls dashed that plan.

"Me and my wife were going to the movies, but I guess I can hook up with you," he told Dee Dee when she called with an urgent request to meet.

"Meet me in the Target parking lot in North Lakeland," she said.

"Well, I'm in Bartow, so I can't be there right away,

but I'll be there in about forty-five minutes to an hour," Greg countered. Although he was actually only a few blocks away from the proposed rendezvous point, Greg needed time to alert investigators Wallace and Clark of the upcoming meeting so they could get in place to monitor activities.

After hanging up with Dee Dee, Greg immediately called Dave Wallace about the impending rendezvous, then bundled himself up against the weather in a sweater and hooded sweatshirt, and raced to the nearby shopping center to meet the detectives. Realizing that the extra layers of clothes would allow him to keep his trusty tape recorder on his person this time, Greg plopped the device in the breast pocket of his shirt beneath the hoodie rather than in the well-worn Red Bull can. From a neighboring lot, Greg and the investigators watched as Dee Dee arrived, driving a car none of them had seen her in before. Greg then counted off another fifteen minutes before exiting so Dee Dee could see him approach the Target lot from the direction he would have driven had he actually been coming from Bartow. Little details like that mattered, he knew, because, ironically enough, Dee Dee was prone to make an issue of anything that didn't add up, and keeping her trust was his only hope of breaking her.

"Man, what in the hell is going on?" he asked as Dee Dee got into his car.

"Judy said that her phone's being tapped, and that they're trying to get her for conspiracy, which she hasn't done anything, Greg. She hasn't done any damn thing. And so she can't talk on her phone no more; she wants a prepaid phone."

Dee Dee rambled on about how Judy's power of attorney was wholly legitimate and that detectives were trying to intimidate the other woman in order "to try to stir some shit up." Then without skipping a beat, Dee Dee shifted gears entirely.

"That is cool," she said, tugging at Greg's jacket. "You gonna wear that in the movie?"

"Yeah, yeah. This my gig," Greg said, accustomed to Dee Dee's non sequiturs.

"Yeah, well, but she said, 'They're trying to stir shit up' and, uh, 'They're trying to do that on purpose.' So she said, 'You know,' and I told her, I said, 'They're just trying to get you just to get you to say something, just, you know, to change the story or anything else.' So she says, 'Well, I want to get rid of my phone and I'm not going to use it anymore. I'm going to use another phone.'"

"Uh-huh."

"So, I need you to go in there and get two phones," Dee Dee said, nodding toward a Radio Shack store a few yards away. "Can you do that? One for her and one for me?"

"Okay. You want another line other than what you got?"

"Yeah. I'm going to ditch this prepaid since it's called you so much, and get another prepaid to call you on, so that anybody that has this one like Judy says . . . they can't see where I've been calling you all the time; you see what I mean."

"Okay."

"But, I've only been talking to you because I'm trying to find Abraham."

"Exactly. Well, hey, I'm all in, baby."

Suddenly, Dee Dee turned misty.

"I love you," she told Greg, weeping. "I've never been so scared in my life."

"Aw, I told you, suck it up and be strong. We in this shit together. I'm, as you see, I'm all in. I can't go no-fucking-where." At that moment, however, Greg was itching to be anywhere but in a small car with this blathering troublemaker.

"How do you do this to somebody's life?" Dee Dee whined before launching into a rant about alleged police harassment. She had done nothing to bring the cops breathing down her neck, she told Greg, but then suggested what he should say should investigators discover their association and come calling on him.

"I wouldn't let you just say 'No comment,'" said Dee Dee, as if she was doing Greg a favor. "You really was talking to a guy named Ronald that talks to Abraham and they were telling you to do all this shit, not me. It was never me. Ronald would come up there and tell you to go down the road to meet him."

This was the first time Greg had heard about this "Ronald" character. Whether he was real, a figment of Dee Dee's wild imagination, or part of her knowing lies, he couldn't tell. But he got the message. If his and Dee Dee's collusion was ever discovered, he was to insist that he was only passing on information to her about Abraham that he had learned from "Ronald." Greg found the woman's twisted mind disgusting, but at the same time, he was fascinated by it. What would she think of next? Mindful that he had a job to do and that detectives had his back, Greg played along with this new scheme.

"All I ever talked to you about is my loan," Greg interjected. "I'm trying to get my loan straight. That's it. I mean, they can't tell . . ."

"You were trying to make me, kept trying to make me an offer so I'd settle because you don't want to be tied with all your shit . . ."

"I don't want to be tied up in this shit. That's it. They can't tie me to this shit man. I'm a little bit smarter than that."

"Just don't let them lie to you 'cause they'll lie and say they know, they know and you know how that goes."

Just as abruptly as they had begun, Dee Dee's waterworks ended.

"Okay, can you get two like this," she asked, grabbing Greg's flip phone. "I like this phone. This is pretty." Dee Dee peeled off $400 for the cell-phone purchases.

As he stepped out of his car into the brisk air, Greg bristled at the cold. He shimmied a wool cap onto his head, zipped his sweatshirt, and pulled up the hood. He tapped the shirt pocket beneath the sweatshirt to make sure the tape recorder was there.

The blonde, middle-aged clerk at the Radio Shack nearly jumped out of her skin when Greg walked in.

"Okay, can I help you sir?" she said in a nervous breath. Her eyes were wide with fright.

"Oh, don't get scared. I see you scared," Greg said, chuckling.

"Yeah," she said, appearing to relax a bit.

"It's just cold outside," Greg explained, indicating his outfit. "I just want to get two of these here." He pointed out the display model that looked most like the phone Dee Dee had admired in the car. Reassured that Greg had come in to conduct business, not robbery, the clerk grew chatty, explaining the pros and cons of various cell phones and their comparative costs. As she relaxed, Greg teased her a little. "I see I came in with my skully on and you was like . . ."

"Oh yeah," said the clerk, with a giggle. "'Cause I've been robbed at gunpoint before."

"I ain't gone rob you, baby."

"Know what that man got? Eighty bucks."

"Well, I ain't trying to rob you, you feel me?"

"Oh no, but he came in with his shirt, trying to hold it up like this."

"Hell, it's cold as hell out there."

They spoke a little more about the phones.

"I couldn't talk you into the 465?" the saleswoman asked.

"Nah," said Greg.

"Looks more like a BlackBerry. It's going to hold up a lot better than these."

"Let me get one of each," Greg said, relenting. "I think my daughter seen somebody with that little phone right there. That's why I say, get one of each." The clerk rang up the two phones and activated each one.

Greg took the phones and sprinted back to his car, tapping on the window for Dee Dee to unlock his door.

"Shit, it's cold as a mother out here," he said, handing her the purchases.

Dee Dee fiddled with the phones Greg had bought, but her thoughts were already on to the next thing. She needed to fabricate a letter from Abraham to his mother, she said. A letter to reassure Elizabeth Walker that her son was all right and would soon be home. She just needed a place to write it in private and off the beaten path.

"Hey, I can go rent a hotel room!" she said excitedly, as if impressed by her own ingenuity.

"If you want me to, I'll come where you're at," Greg offered.

"You go rent it for me," Dee Dee said, explaining that she would drop off Judy's new phone while Greg secured a room at the Comfort Inn, "the nice" motel behind a nearby McDonald's. Greg was to register the room under the names of Mark and Mary Weeks and get two keys—one for himself and the other for Dee Dee, which he would deliver to her later that afternoon. They would meet back at the motel around 5:00 or 6:00 P.M. and work on the letter together. When it was done, she and Greg would drive by Ms. Walker's house and place it in her mailbox.

"I'm going to go to the hotel and I'm going to write that fucker and I'm going to throw it in there and that's it," Dee Dee said. Then she switched subjects yet again.

"I want the police to know what Cedric is telling me.

And I think it's a bunch of bull. Cedric is telling me that he talked to Abraham and Abraham told him to give him that house. And he wants me to sign the house over to him. And I think that's something that the cops need to know. So if he's talking to Abraham, the cops need to know that. And they fucking need to watch him. Cedric said that he seen Abraham after the ninth and ABC News didn't report it. So I want to know the truth."

"One thing about it," Greg said, "we're fixing to find out."

"So if I put that in there, we'll find out who is telling the truth and who is lying," Dee Dee continued. "And at least they'll investigate it, and that will buy me another week so I can plan this."

Who knew what to believe when it came to Dee Dee and Cedric? Each had used the other—Dee Dee getting Cedric to foster lies about Abraham's status; Cedric cashing in on Dee Dee's need for a lackey to do some of her dirty work. And both were habitual but clumsy liars. Once detectives began snooping around on the case, unnerving Abraham's friends, family, and debtors, Cedric publicly denied ever filing the missing-person's report, insisting that someone else must have done it. Police say he was "uncooperative and confrontational" after that. Beyond ironic, it was downright idiotic that Dee Dee would be so dogged about getting the truth out of a man whose main value to her had been his willingness to lie.

With assistance from the two watchful detectives, who had apprised the motel's managers of their surveillance activity, Greg paid for one room for one night and obtained two keys, one of which he put into Dee Dee's hand in a quick exchange in a Waffle House parking lot.

"See you 'round six o'clock," Greg said, driving off.

As accustomed as he was to bizarre and unexpected behavior when it came to Dee Dee Moore, Greg was not prepared for his greeting at the motel room later that night. Opening the door, Dee Dee looked almost like a HAZMAT technician, covered head to toe in protective gear—plastic gloves on her hands, a cap covering her hair, a medical mask covering her nose and mouth, and disposable covers on her shoes.

"Put these on," Dee Dee directed, tossing gloves, mask, and shoe covers at Greg. "I don't want any of our DNA on anything in here."

Speechless, Greg complied, at first dumbfounded by the sight of Dee Dee dressed like a surgeon, but now alarmed.

This motherfucker about to murder me, he thought. *Lord, I ain't got no pistol; my knife's in the car. And I got to fight this big motherfucker. She's fixing to murder me and nobody gonna know I'm in here but Wallace and them. They might get her, but bitch, I ain't ready to die.*

Greg suited up without taking his eyes off Dee Dee or turning his back to her. A surge of panic hit him when she reached under the bed. He breathed a sigh of relief as she pulled out a box containing a brand-new laptop computer. Next she pulled a box containing a new printer from behind the bed's headboard and loaded it with white paper from a new package. Together, Greg and Dee Dee connected the two devices and Dee Dee began typing.

"Dear Mom," she started. She hammered away at the missive for an hour, stopping periodically to read aloud what she had written thus far, concerned about tone as much as accuracy.

"Does that sound like Abraham?" she asked Greg repeatedly. "'Cause this needs to be as believable as possible."

When at last Dee Dee was satisfied that she had said enough, she printed out her work and handed it to Greg for one last review. He scanned the letter but paid scant attention to it since all he could think about was how he wanted to get the hell out of that room. He couldn't help but be amazed, however, by how long and detailed the letter was. But, then, why would he expect anything less from Dee Dee, with her annoying tendency to talk too much and repeat herself, not to mention her talent for making up stories?

The letter said:

I like being missing just not all over the news. I been through a lot, mom. You know it. I'm just tired. Over where I stayed, no one knows me and there are so many out-of-towners you never run into the same people twice except the police. I got a new one that Dee Dee will like for her book. The officer that's around my neighborhood kept bugging and teasing me. I look like Abraham Shakespeare. I showed him my fake ID and it worked until last week when he caught me for speeding. I was scared so I told him the truth. He never ran my driver's license. I just explained all that I've been through and admitted to him who I was. He followed me home and I paid him twenty grand to keep his mouth shut. He going to look out for me now. He said anybody doubt who you are, just call me.

Greg shook his head as if to shake loose his confusion, then went back to reading.

Dee's mad because I won't come back but I can't right now. I see where it's been hard on her 15 year old son. Tell R. J., her son, I will buy him a car and send him money in the mail for what I put his mom through. I don't want him mad at me when I come back.

I told Torrie she not going to get a damn dime. Dee tell people she won't go to jail for me on child support. I like my new life too much to sit in jail 179 days. I guess tell Judy to go to court and find out how much that bitch going to cost me. Torrie said I had stink ass breath and acted like she only slept with me for the money and got pregnant on purpose. The court won't even let me get a DNA test when she told that guy it not even my baby. I so upset to talk to you, mom. I almost killed that girl and if I come back, I think she will try to put me in jail. If she truly did not press charges, she said someone needs to stop me. I need to get help. But I still want to hear from you with all that mess. Thanks for letting me talk the other day.

Why did they say you have not talked to me since April? I called you two days after Christmas. No one forgets their son's voice. Why are you going this way? You know it was me and if I don't have a warrant, they cannot force me to come see you. I will see you, I promise, just give me some time. I'm trying to locate this girl and make sure she's not going to start some shit.

I only called because Dee lied and put the word out that you were in the hospital with chest pains because of all of this. I really don't feel like talking about what all I did yet. When I get some help and work it out myself, I will come back and explain to you.

I still can't write a letter. This good friend typing for me. I don't want everyone to know my business so I can't say some things to you. You let me to be raised by my dad for years. You should understand more than anyone I just need time.

This bitch has sure covered all the bases, Greg thought, reading on.

Don't worry about Dee. If she goes to jail she will be okay. The charges won't stick. There are too many people that know I left. I gave her enough money. She knew what to expect. She should have not got involved. So now she just have to deal with it. She would not take anything from me unless I agreed to retire you. She was the only one that helped me when my money was messed up. Don't feel bad for what Dee going through. I gave her 10x what she did for me. I hope you got to put in a notice at work now.

The letter went on for four more pages, with "Abraham" insisting that he was "not a child and I'm not out of my mind"; that he wanted Dee Dee to give Cedric Edom the deed to the house so that Cedric would shut up and go away; that he wanted Judy Haggins to do his taxes; that he would "never forgive" his older brother for threatening to kill him; that he would ask "Ronald" to drop by and pick up the framed newspaper article about his lottery win if Dee Dee would locate it and place it on her back porch.

"I only wrote you just in case you really worried. Just in case you can't keep this to yourself and you really worried about me, here is a Christmas present to you."

"That sounds good," Greg said. "That's good. You can write a damn book. That's a good one. The whole letter is good."

"Okay," Dee Dee said.

"The whole fucking letter is good."

"I want her to think . . . I want to make it look that he doesn't give a shit if he went to jail or not."

Another hour passed in the overheated room, where a jittery white woman and an apprehensive black man decked out in surgical gear collaborated to forge a letter intended to convince an elderly woman that everything was alright with her beleaguered, illiterate son who happened to be a millionaire, and who also happened to be missing and presumed dead.

"How do you like the twenty grand for the police?" Dee Dee asked merrily. "That's something that he would do because he owes five thousand for that other—"

"That's good," Greg said, interrupting. "That's good."

"And I didn't put too much where he—"

Greg interrupted again, cautioning Dee Dee not to get too "flamboyant" with the letter, or to mention herself too often. "The more you do to it, the more you're incriminating what you're doing," he told her.

Greg knew that Dee Dee's tendency to go on and on, covering every issue and every detail, was likely to only help the case. Guilty people often overtalk, digging the hole deeper. But, at that moment, he just wanted to finish with this dirty business, ditch the mask and gloves, and exit the sweltering room.

As the final version slid from the printer, Dee Dee lifted each page with a pair of tweezers, carefully folded the letter, and placed it in an envelope with her gloved hands. She filled an envelope sealer with water and dabbed the envelope flap. Better that than to lick the adhesive or dampen it with her finger and leave her DNA on the paper. Then the pair grabbed towels to wipe down anything and everything they might have touched in the room even with their gloved hands.

Greg helped Dee Dee clear the room and load the laptop and printer into the trunk of her car. He was to follow her in his car to Elizabeth Walker's house. But several blocks down the road, Dee Dee parked her car and told Greg that she would drive his car the rest of the way.

"Does it really sound good?" Dee Dee asked him again about the letter. "It doesn't sound like it came from me?"

"No, it doesn't sound like it came from you," Greg said. "That's why I told you not to keep digging yourself in it. Let yourself go; you know what I'm saying? Leave yourself alone and emphasize on something else."

As Greg's Camry approached Elizabeth Walker's neighborhood, Dee Dee stopped the car about a block short of the house and instructed Greg to walk the rest of the way and place the letter in Ms. Walker's mailbox. Greg lifted the envelope with his gloved hands and trudged up the block. He paused briefly at the curbside mailbox and glanced around quickly for any prying eyes, then carefully laid the envelope inside.

"We got that done," he said, back at the car, pulling off the plastic gloves at last. "The letter is in."

He felt relieved that this ridiculous deceit was over, although Dee Dee continued to get on his nerves, babbling about her worries that traffic cameras might have captured them together in the car.

Once Dee Dee and Greg were out of sight, Detectives Wallace and Clark pulled up to the Walker house, opened the mailbox door, and removed the counterfeit letter, placing it into an evidence bag for its ride to the PCSO evidence room.

CHAPTER ELEVEN

· · · · ·

Sheriff Grady Judd was renowned for not pulling punches, sometimes not even when political correctness, civil sensibilities, or even common courtesy required it. Once, when asked why his SWAT team had shot an undocumented immigrant sixty-eight times after the man had allegedly fatally shot a deputy, Judd told the *Orlando Sentinel,* "That's all the bullets we had, or we would have shot him more."

Reporters who convened for Judd's January 13, 2010, news conference about Abraham Shakespeare were assured of walking out with a good story that day, not only because of how colorful they knew the sheriff to be, but also because rumors and innuendo about Abraham's mysterious disappearance had been swirling around Florida for months now, and this was their chance to nail the story down factually and in official context. The day before, Judd had officially named Dorice Donegan Moore a "person of interest" in the disappearance of Abraham Lee Shakespeare, a designation that, notwithstanding legal translations, meant "suspect" to most people.

Dressed in his black sheriff's uniform, Judd stepped to the lectern and got straight to the point with a pithy opening statement.

"It appears, and I'm very cautious, that Abraham Shakespeare is broke," he said. "Two and a half years ago, a little less than three years ago, he had $12,700,000 and it appears that he's broke. The investigation's ongoing."

The news that Abraham had burned through millions and millions of dollars in so short a time was surprising, but indeed, even before Dee Dee came into the picture, Abraham had already given away, spent, or squandered the majority of his winnings. Only about one million in cash and three million in assets were left by the time she took over. Even so, Dee Dee had gotten her hands on all of that remaining money by April of 2009, leaving the accounts in Abraham's name empty.

"We certainly hope that the confidence act that Dee Dee Moore is involved in to make it appear that Abraham Shakespeare has disappeared with money is correct and he's alive and well," Judd continued. "But our investigation doesn't lead us to believe that at this time. It leads us to believe that she pulled a con game on Shakespeare, convinced him to move his assets into a joint account through an LLC that she named Abraham

Shakespeare, LLC but created access to. Plus she agreed to buy the house and other assets from him, for which we can't find any records of purchase."

Though he did not go into detail at the news conference, Judd's investigative staff had plowed through years of Dee Dee's financial records and found that between March 9, 2005, and January 7, 2009, American Medical Professionals had profits totaling just under $721,000—well short of the amount Dee Dee said she paid for Abraham's house and asset portfolio, and that was if she hadn't spent a penny on food, clothing, utilities, mortgages, car payments or other living expenses over the five years.

"She made the statement, and she agreed with this, that, 'Oh, I paid him that $840,000 in cash.'" Judd continued. "I'm sure the IRS is going to be interested in that. And we're going to make sure that they know that she apparently had $800,000, according to her statement, that she gave Abraham in cash. Quite frankly, we don't see where she had $840,000."

The sheriff wound down his statement with a reminder that the reward for information leading to Shakespeare's whereabouts had been doubled since the offer was first posted on December 1.

"That's $10,000 to find Abraham Shakespeare dead or alive, and we don't ask anyone to testify or put themselves in that position," he said. He recited the toll-free number for tipsters to call, anonymously if they wanted.

"We certainly hope Abraham's alive and well and he has successfully hidden himself away. But none of the circumstances and none of the investigation we've completed up to this point leads us to believe he's still alive."

It wasn't the first time journalists had heard someone speculate that Abraham Shakespeare was dead. But it was the first time an official had said so publicly. They had their story. A big one.

Even as an officially named person of interest in an active homicide case, Dee Dee still had her freedom physically, but Sheriff Judd's incriminating news conference caged her in dread and worry. Why hadn't all of her hard work at diverting attention away from herself done the trick? Why hadn't Judd mentioned the letter to Abraham's mother? Why hadn't there been any talk around town about it? After all, she had gone to great lengths to make sure it sounded legit, that it could not be traced to her, and that it got to Elizabeth Walker herself. The letter was supposed to put a damper on the rumor and doubts. Instead, investigators were turning up the heat, publicly incriminating her.

"Miz Elizabeth should have filed a police report by now about that letter she got from Abraham," Dee Dee said in a frantic phone call to Greg. "I don't understand why the investigators keep pushing this thing when Abraham's own mother has said she's heard from the man." If the stakes hadn't been so high, Greg would have chuckled to himself over Dee Dee's breakdown. She had no way of knowing how her insidious scheme had failed; that Elizabeth Walker had never received the phony letter because detectives had gotten it first. Now she was squirming, frustrated as all get-out that nothing had come of her diabolical vision of journalists and law enforcement officials telling the world that, lo and behold, the missing man was not missing after all—and there had been no word of Abraham's mother receiving a long, detailed letter from him explaining his voluntary absence. Although he knew he would have to help pick up the pieces of Dee Dee's broken psyche yet again, for the moment, Greg was enjoying her defeat and his role in foiling her plan.

"Did you see what Grady Judd said about me on the news, that I'm a person of interest and that they think Abraham is dead?" Dee Dee squealed.

"Fuck all that," Greg said, stepping back in character as Dee Dee's intrepid co-conspirator. "They don't have a body."

"Yeah, but that doesn't seem to matter to these assholes. They're just trying to pin something on me and I haven't done nothing to the man. I would never, ever do anything to hurt another human being. All I have ever done is try to help Abraham, and Grady Judd wants to say I'm a person of interest?"

"Like I said, fuck all that. They don't have no hard evidence."

"But Abraham's own mother just heard from him that he's fine and that he's going to come back soon. She got a letter from him and all."

Greg felt a wave of disgust that Dee Dee would keep

saying such things to him of all people and with such
conviction. She knew he knew that the letter was fake—
he'd been there when she wrote it. He'd helped her
deliver it. Was there no end to her wickedness? For
months, she had made his head spin with an assortment
of conflicting, suspicious stories about Abraham's whereabouts. He'd wanted to believe her in the beginning
when she said Shakyboy was in Puerto Rico or Texas or
Jamaica or on another cruise. He had indulged her con-
tinuous rants about imaginary drug dealers who had
lured Abraham into their lairs with outlandish promises
of doubling or tripling his money in exchange for a large
investment in their underworld trade. He had feigned
sympathy when Dee Dee had cried about harassment,
intimidation, and threats from the mysterious Ronald,
including her claims that Ronald had been leaving
threatening notes at the back door. He had kept his
mouth shut when he wanted to scream, *"Fool, don't you
remember that 'Ronald' is the name you told me to use
when I called you from one of those cell phones you had me
buy?"* He had pretended to be alarmed and outraged
that "Ronald" had called Dee Dee's adolescent son to let
her know that he was watching the boy, insinuating that
R. J. would be harmed or killed if Dee Dee ever told
police about him and his ties to Abraham. Greg even
feigned support for Dee Dee's fiction about Abraham
dodging the police because of an altercation with an
underage prostitute, going so far as to tell Dee Dee that
he had a friend checking into whether charges had been

filed so that Abraham would know whether or not the coast was clear for him to come home. Greg had restrained himself when Dee Dee pissed him off by proposing that he make yet another phone call about a bogus Abraham sighting, this time to a reporter at the *St. Petersburg Times*, calmly persuading her to nix that. Without telling her how nuts she was, he had listened to her muse about planting a rumor that Abraham was among the 200,000 killed in the catastrophic earthquake that devastated Haiti in 2010, a preposterous claim even by Dee Dee Moore's abysmal standards.

But for her to talk to him about the counterfeit letter as if it were legitimate took Greg's distrust of and disdain for her to a whole new level. *Does she not remember that I was with her when she wrote the fake letter to Mrs. Walker?* he wondered. *Has she forgotten that I was the one who put the phony letter in Abraham's mother's mailbox? That I watched her work on a brand-new computer and a brand-new printer so there wouldn't be any trace of the underhandedness on her home equipment? That I put on that crazy mask and gloves and shit just like her? That I rented the hotel room for her to do all the dirty work in? And she has the nerve to claim to me that Abraham's mother just heard from him, like it's the truth? How delusional is this chick?*

He hung up the phone, stunned that Dee Dee Moore could be *that* off her rocker.

"This bitch is out of her mind," he told his wife. "But I gotta go through with this shit to get to the truth."

"You got to be careful, Greg," Likicha said. "You got to watch your back every minute."

"Every second," Greg said somberly.

In stark contrast to the rattled figure he had spoken to earlier that day, Greg found a smiling, cheerful Dee Dee waiting for him at a service station in Plant City. Only hours before, she seemed on the verge of a complete breakdown. Now, there was a bounce in her step as she walked toward Greg's car.

"Abraham's back!" she said giddily. "Somebody told me they just saw him in Walden Lake! I went by the house myself and saw his car!"

"For real?" Greg said, surprised by this absurd new tact and Dee Dee's emotional about-face. For a moment, it crossed his mind that Dee Dee's lightheartedness might have some merit. She did appear genuinely relieved and excited. True or not, he knew he had to go along.

"Come get in my car and we'll go over there. I'm gonna find his ass," she said.

Dee Dee drove quickly toward the Plant City subdivision where she once lived. As she approached one large house, she slowed the car.

"Damn!" she said. "The fucker's gone. I came by here before and his car was there. He got away!"

"You sure this was the right street?" Greg asked innocently, though in reality he was now convinced that this was nothing but another one of Dee Dee's wild-goose chases.

"Greg, I saw the car myself and I saw a figure through the window that looked like Abraham. I don't know he got away so fast."

"Well, we need to get away from in front of these people's house."

"Okay, okay. But where do you think Abraham went?"

"How the hell would I know?"

"I know, but he was right here just a little while ago. I'm going to catch his ass next time."

As she drove off, Dee Dee seemed more encouraged than disappointed.

"Aren't you happy, though?" she asked Greg. "I hope this is all over. I'll know tomorrow. But until then, I'm on pins and needles."

"If he show up, fine. If he don't, I'm gonna deal with it."

"I'm excited. I'm gonna go home and see if they have any press conferences . . ."

"Who told you Abraham was here?"

"This guy told me that his mama said that she had seen him. He had called me back and I had told him, 'If you ever run into Abraham again, let him know his mom's sick.' And I guess he ran into him again. We'll know tomorrow."

Greg shook his head. Either Dee Dee Moore was the best friend Abraham Shakespeare ever had, refusing to give up on him, or she was the most demented scam artist he had ever seen.

Word began to spread through town that, after nine months of unexplained absence, Abraham had at long last returned to central Florida, raising Dee Dee's hopes that her long ordeal with the detectives was over. For days, she poured over the newspapers and watched local newscasts, eager for an official report that Abraham was back in town. But not a word was said about it in the media.

Greg knew no such reports were forthcoming because there was no truth to the story. Once again, Dee Dee had made up a lie, and despite her confidence that it would pour cold water on the investigation and get detectives off her back, Greg knew Dave Wallace, David Clark, and Chris Lynn were far too smart to fall for it.

He also knew the media silence would send Dee Dee back to the drawing board. He braced himself for another desperate call from her, as sure to come as the Florida sun.

"There hasn't been nothing on the news," Dee Dee whimpered into the phone. "I don't understand. All these people have been hearing from Abraham lately and his mama has a letter from him saying he was coming home and now he's back, but there's not a word from the sheriff's office or in the news about it."

"Those rumors been going around so long that nobody believes them until they see Abraham with their own two eyes," Greg countered.

"But he's back. I know because I saw his car at that house."

"That don't matter. You been saying that he's all right and was coming back and the police don't believe you. They ain't 'bout to go on no wild-goose chase."

"But it's not a wild-goose chase, Greg. It's not. But, you know what, you're right about them not believing me, because I've been telling them about the drug dealers too and they won't follow up on that either. The one time they did, they told the guy that I said he had threatened me, which puts me and my family in more danger. They don't care. They just want to make me the fall guy for Abraham not being around."

"Well, you need your own fall guy."

"What do you mean?"

In a brainstorming session days before, Wallace and Clark had come up with the idea of offering a scapegoat to Dee Dee to see where she might go with it. Greg had agreed to feel Dee Dee out on it, suggesting that he would tell her he had a relative who was about to begin a long prison sentence, and that with a payoff from Dee Dee, the man would say that he killed Abraham.

"You need somebody who will take this case for you, take the rap," he said.

"Who would do that?" Dee Dee asked. "And why?"

"You get somebody who's already going in to do a lot of time and cut a deal with them that you'll hook 'em up." Greg told Dee Dee that such a patsy would probably require that she keep money in his inmate account so that, whenever he wanted, he could buy whatever snacks, sundries, and other goods he wanted from the prison canteen.

"Is that all?" Dee Dee asked. "Just take care of his canteen?"

"What deal you cut is between you and him," Greg

said. "I'm just saying there are people who will do this for you and get the heat off us." Greg made a point of saying "us" and "we" whenever he could in hopes of reassuring Dee Dee that he was on her side and understood the gravity and urgency of the situation. Dee Dee eagerly took the bait.

"Do you know someone who would do that for me?"

"Yeah, I got a cousin who's about to do twenty-five years in a plea deal."

"You trust him?"

"I told you, he's my cousin. You ought to know I wouldn't bring in somebody I don't trust. It's good that I've been in the kind of trouble I been in, 'cause you need the most orneriest type of man you can find and I know these dudes. They my partners."

"Okay. And you'll ask him about doing this for me? For us?"

"I'm gonna call him soon as we hang up."

"Okay, 'cause I'm really worried, Greg. Ronald kept threatening me and telling me that Abraham was okay. But I don't believe he's okay anymore because he won't let me talk to him."

"Well, let me get in touch with my partner and I'll let you know."

CHAPTER TWELVE

■■■■■

Greg could tell from Dee Dee's excitement that the fall-guy proposal held promise. He couldn't wait to tell Detectives Wallace and Clark how Dee Dee had lit up as he unveiled the plan. Greg even offered to find the perfect person to play the role of confessor for hire.

But Wallace and Clark had their own actor in mind. They knew the type they were looking for from the old days when they were in narcotics and worked closely with undercover officers. Clark knew that Mike Smith, an eleven-year veteran with the police department in Lake Wales, was widely admired for his undercover work. Smith had served with Clark on the federal task force that broke the Carlton Potts murder case back in 2006. He was confident that Smith could sell the mercenary bit to Dee Dee, and he pumped his fist in the air when his old cohort agreed to do it.

Abraham Shakespeare in October 2006, less than one month before he won the $31 million Florida lottery.

The spacious, modern home in North Lakeland that Abraham bought for himself with his winnings.

Dorice "Dee Dee" Moore, the woman Abraham hoped would help him handle his finances.

The family room of the luxury home Abraham Shakespeare bought for himself. After Abraham disappeared, Dee Dee moved into the house with her son and boyfriend, claiming she had purchased the house from Abraham.

Surveillance photos of Dee Dee Moore meeting with Greg Smith in his car at a Lakeland parking lot. Polk County Sheriff's Office investigators were watching Greg when Dee Dee showed up.

Sentorria "Torrie" Butler, the mother of Abraham's second son, Jeremiyah, who was born in 2008.

Abraham's younger cousin Cedric Edom, the family member who first reported Abraham missing.

The house on State Road 60 in Plant City where Dee Dee Moore ran her medical staffing business, where her boyfriend's mother lived, and where Abraham Shakespeare was murdered.

Dee Dee Moore provided this truck and trailer to Greg Smith for use in moving Abraham Shakespeare's buried remains off of her property.

A sheriff's investigator surveys a large concrete slab in the backyard of Dee Dee Moore's house. A day later, Abraham Shakespeare's remains were unearthed about six feet below the slab.

A sheriff's investigator measures the depth of Abraham Shakespeare's makeshift grave beneath the concrete slab in Dee Dee's backyard.

An aerial photo of Dee Dee's properties on State Road 60 in Plant City. Abraham was killed in the house with the paintball field behind it, and was buried behind the house next door (in the lower part of the photo).

The office safe where Dee Dee claims she kept tens of thousands of dollars as well as the gun she said was used to kill Abraham.

Assistant state's attorney Jay Pruner portrayed Dee Dee Moore as a greedy and conniving manipulator. DEBORAH MATHIS

An undercover officer was not who Greg had in mind though, and as tactfully as he knew how, he told Wallace and Clark that he wasn't comfortable bringing in someone he didn't know—someone who might make a mess of all the progress he had made in getting Dee Dee to open up, someone who might spook her. The detectives assured him that Smith could pull off the pretense without endangering the case or scaring Dee Dee off. Mike Smith knew what he was doing, they said, and he would be wired so that they could listen in on the conversation in real time.

Reluctantly, Greg agreed—what else could he do?—and reminded the officers that, in anticipation of Dee Dee's skittishness and paranoia, he had already told her that his cousin was going to do the deal.

"So tell [the] dude not to act like he don't know me," Greg directed. "He got to go along with us knowing each other a long time."

"Got it," said Wallace.

The meeting with Mike Smith was set for two days later in the Lakeside Mall parking lot. Greg and Dee Dee would be there, he assured detectives.

"So will we," Clark said.

"Here's the deal," Greg said as Dee Dee got into his car the next day. "He say, 'Okay, I'll do this.'"

Dee Dee gasped with delight.

"I said, 'Well, man, listen, what this person needs is that, she wants to know if you will take a fall if anything goes wrong saying that you did something to somebody and you tossed they ass in Tampa Bay or somewhere, any-where,'" Greg said breathlessly. "So, he was like, 'Yeah.' He say, 'But listen, the only way I'm doing this shit is because of you,' he said. 'I'm facing time anyway.'"

The prospective fall guy was facing twenty-five years in prison on drug charges, Greg explained, telling Dee Dee that his cousin had nothing to lose by saying he had offed someone since he was going to be locked up for a long time anyway. There was just one condition: the fall guy wanted to make sure his family was taken care of financially.

And one more thing: he would need the body.

"What he said was, 'I want to make sure this mother-fucker gone,'" Greg reported. "He wants this bitch to be gone. He don't want him to surface 'cause if he sur-face, it's gone fuck him up."

"Why would it fuck him up? Because then he would get off," Dee Dee pushed back. "They'll be like, 'Wow, you alive.'"

No, Greg told her, then they'd just get him for lying. Dee Dee countered that he could claim to have simply *thought* the guy was Abraham.

Greg was getting frustrated by Dee Dee's pushback. *Here I am trying to explain to this woman that I got some-one willing to say he killed Abraham Shakespeare and who just wants to make sure Abraham ain't going to show up some day and create a shit storm and you're hung up on what kind of lie to tell if things go wrong? And such a stu-pid lie, at that. Homeboy shouldn't tell authorities that he hasn't killed anyone after all? He supposed to tell them he was mistaken about* who *he had killed? Are you out of your ever-lovin' mind?*

Just as Greg pondered how to put a lid on that can of worms, Dee Dee shifted gears.

"He could cop a deal," she said of the fall guy.

"Well," said Greg, "I told him, 'Listen, what you do is, this the way this gone have to go: you gonna have to say Abraham came to you trying to buy some dope. He purchased some dope from you. And when he came back to pay you, because you knew who he was and you knew that he should have had the money, that he came to you and said he didn't have all the money. And you gave him ample enough time to get the money and you told him to come see you and talk to you about it and everything was straight. And when he got there, y'all did what you did.' How does that sound?"

"Yeah," said Dee Dee, sitting up in her seat. "'Cause I wouldn't give him the money. 'Cause he wanted the money out of checking and I wouldn't give him the money."

Greg watched the excitement spread across Dee Dee's face and stuck his hook in deeper. "He the type of person, I'm gonna let you know right now," he told her of his pretend cousin, "like if he's in something, like I'm in this shit with you, he's in."

Dee Dee lunged toward Greg and wrapped her arms around his neck.

"You are such an exceptional person," she said sweetly. "You know, when we're eighty years old, we got to sit down and write a book. We got to write a book about this shit."

"What you need to do right now is get your shit lined up," Greg said, pulling back from Dee Dee's embrace.

"You are awesome," she cooed, hugging him again. When she pulled back, Greg saw fat tears cresting in her eyes. "Greg, look at me," Dee Dee said. "I haven't done anything. And I'm fucking screwed because of the money. And like my lawyer said, 'You're fucking screwed; you're gonna go to jail because of the money.' That's not fair." She was now in full cry mode. "Why are you being so nice to me?" she whimpered.

"Hell, look what you did for me," Greg replied.

"I know, but . . . So nice. So nice."

"Like I told you from the beginning, I'm in with you. I'm here all the fuckin' way."

January 21, 2010, broke clear, bright, sunny, and cool over Plant City as Greg set out to meet Dee Dee. The meeting with Mike Smith was a couple of hours off, and Greg wanted to get to Lakeside Mall early to brief Dee Dee on how to proceed with this man who was going to make a false confession so that she could have some peace.

No sooner had they said hello than Dee Dee launched into a monologue. She had been thinking all night about the fall-guy plan and had had a brainstorm: What if she could produce the gun used to shoot Abraham and somehow tie it to the fall guy? Wouldn't that make his confession all the more believable?

"The gun!" Greg exclaimed. It was the first he'd heard about Abraham being shot. He hadn't expected anything like that and didn't know where Dee Dee was going with it, but he was damn sure going to find out. "With his fingerprints on it?" Greg mused. "That would be easier for him to take the fucking case. And that would bring the heat off you strong."

Dee Dee looked pleased with herself for having come up with an idea that Greg seemed to think was smart.

"He needs to bury that motherfucker after he's put his hands on it," Greg said, suggesting that it would help the fall guy seem more legit if he could tell police later where he ditched the weapon. "You don't want to tie yourself to that gun no kinda fuckin' way."

"But it's registered to me," Dee Dee said.

Greg felt a rush of excitement. He was about to get his hands on a vital piece of evidence. He was proud that he had outwitted the con woman and gotten her to trust him this much. He liked proving his value.

"Okay," he said, feeding into Dee Dee's insatiable appetite for alibis and cover-ups. "Then he broke in your fuckin' house. That fuckin' gun. Man, man, man, man, man. Now you made a real fuckin' alibi. That's the way to get your ass outta this. He held everybody up and he went through your shit and found your gun."

"And Abraham pulled a gun on him and he pulled one on Abraham," Dee Dee added.

"Or threatened you that if you say anything about guns or anything, he's gonna kill your child."

"I really don't believe Abraham's okay anymore," Dee Dee said, changing directions as usual. "I think he'd have called me by now. I think that if [his mother] really filed a report that he was okay, I think she was forced. If that's the case, Miz Elizabeth can go to jail for doing that." Once again, Greg did not challenge Dee Dee's delusional assertion about Abraham's mother, who both he and Dee Dee knew had never filed such a report. If Dee Dee wanted to keep playing that game, fine, as long as he could still get that gun from her. But first, he had to entertain more rantings about Ronald, with Dee Dee speculating that the fictional drug dealer might be intimidating Abraham's associates and family, including his mother. She had tried and tried to get investigators to check out the drug-dealer claims, she said, but they had always shrugged her off. Now, Ronald had probably killed Abraham. In fact, she said, she wouldn't be surprised if Ronald had killed and buried him somewhere.

"I can get Ronald to tell me where it is," Dee Dee said.

"Show me where the property at and I'll pick my time and I'll go out there and move that motherfucker," Greg said, sensing that he was getting close to critical information and that he had to be careful not to show the excitement and surprise he was feeling.

"As long as I give them the killer himself, I'm cutting a deal that they can't charge me," she said. Maybe Ronald had not only killed Abraham, but had also buried him on her property to frame her, she said.

Greg felt his pulse race. He knew how Dee Dee worked. She floated incriminating information as a trial balloon—as if it were merely hypothetical—to test his reaction. He knew if he had bolted then or expressed any alarm, she would have insisted that burying Abraham on her property was just a theory. She had always been careful to phrase things in ways that gave her an out.

Dee Dee's indifference to Abraham's fate and her self-absorption left Greg seething inside. But, he knew he had to hide it. He hadn't gotten this far—hadn't gotten this much out of her—to blow it now. He played along.

"You need to talk to fuckin' Ronald," Greg said sternly. "Even if you have to bribe that motherfucker."

"I'll give him one of my houses. Detectives think he's out there on that property."

"You get with Ronald. You tell Ronald whatever the fuck you have to tell him. 'Man, listen, man, I'm fixing to sign this house over to you right now. Tell me where you put him.'"

But Dee Dee worried that the sight, sounds, and smells of digging around on property would pique the neighbors' interest, especially her boyfriend's mother, who lived nearby.

Just then, a white GMC Yukon truck pulled into view. The fall guy had arrived.

Greg helped Dee Dee into the front passenger seat of the big SUV and leaned across her to give the large, bearded, dreadlock-haired driver a hand grip and shake.

"This my baby right here," Greg said to the guy, pointing to Dee Dee. "You got to take care of her, man." He zipped around the back of the car and let himself in to the backseat. "She was scared you would flip over and that you the police," Greg continued, forcing a chuckle. "I told her, man, we don't deal like that."

"Why would you do [this], though, for me?" Dee Dee asked, surveying the stranger in the driver's seat.

"I'm going [to jail] anyhow," he said.

"Well, I tell you, do this and you're going to be a very popular person. You're going to be a legend. You're going to be in a book and probably on the Oprah show. So, you're willing to be on the Oprah show?"

Mike Smith looked straight ahead as the woman chattered on.

"This situation has gotten big. Because of the money that Abraham had transferred to me. He transferred me his assets because Torrie was trying to get him for child support. Well, with him doing so much, he didn't care. Under Matthew 6 or whatever in the Bible, it said to give, give, you know, without nobody knowing. And his problem was that everybody kept coming after him for money, money, money and it baffled him and he just got tired of it."

Mike glanced at the big blonde babbler for a few seconds, then once again fixed his gaze straight ahead.

"So, what happened was, Torrie was trying to get the last of what he had, and what he had left, and he didn't want Torrie to have it be for child support because he feels like she had that baby in vain. Well, since he transferred me that, these cops are trying to frame me for killing Abraham. I really didn't kill the man. But he was dealing with some really big, big-time drug dealers that told him the cash that I gave him to buy the assets that they would take it and triple it three times. And they told him that 'if you bring us your case, we'll triple it three times.' So Abraham said he was gonna go and let them triple it three times."

Greg could sense Mike starting to seethe behind the wheel. Dee Dee's ramblings could be grating and hard to follow. At the same time, it was often hard for Greg not to be intrigued by the web she was spinning. But he was in no mood for Dee Dee's whiny, delusional blather right now, so he stepped out of the truck to have a cigarette.

"I feel like, if Abraham was okay, he would contact me by now because he transferred all that stuff into my name and then he was supposed to leave and, you know, not come back for a while. But he would have come back, he would have come back for Christmastime, and he has not been back. And they're trying to do what they call corpus delicti on me—charging me without a body—because he transferred his assets before he left to me. But I really did not have nothing to do with it. These, these drug dealers told me that if I ever told the cops any of their names and told them that they were with Abraham that night and all, that they would kill my fourteen-year-old-son. They called my son one day on his phone at school to prove to me they knew his number. And the last drug dealers I told the cops about, they went and told the guys that I said that they would kill me and the guys came right back to me. So I came and told the cops about it because they freakin' are big mouths; they don't care if I die or not; they just want Abraham."

At long last, Dee Dee took a breath.

"But, he was supposed to leave and then he was supposed . . . How long was he supposed to be gone for?"

Mike asked. "'Cause it don't make no, it don't make no fuckin' sense for me to go up there and tell these people I did this shit and then he show up."

"He would have come back by now. He was supposed to be back in November for Thanksgiving and he didn't come back. And they keep telling me, the drug dealers keep telling me he's okay and that they'll kill me or kill my son if I tell their name and address. But I don't know their name and address. I don't know them. I just know the guys come up for money at my house before, that's all I know."

Mike shook his head. Dee Dee's theories and schemes were not making sense. "Why would Ronald force me to take a rap for something they fuckin' did?" he asked.

"Because the heat would be brought on him for his gun deals," Dee Dee said. "He does not want, the gun dealers do not want to be found out and I really believe that they're doing something to him . . ." Now, in Dee Dee's account, not only was the fantastical Ronald a drug dealer, but a gunrunner as well.

"My thing is, if [Abraham] ain't dead, it don't make no sense, 'cause he's gonna show up and then what?" Mike interjected. "Do they have insurance on him?"

"No. He has no insurance."

"Okay. That's gonna be the next thing they come up with."

Indeed, detectives had done a thorough search for life-insurance policies on Abraham Shakespeare early in the investigation, well aware that many a murder victim was offed by a beneficiary who wanted to get his or her hands on the proceeds. "Since November '09, I have followed the money trail and feel certain that [Abraham Shakespeare] would not have purchased a life insurance policy on himself," Detective Lynn said in a letter to one of the many major insurance underwriters he contacted in his search. "However, it would behoove us to know if someone else may possibly benefit from the individual being labeled deceased." But no policy was ever found insuring Abraham's life.

"They're charging me without a body because he transferred so much money over into my name," Dee Dee continued. "He transferred a bunch of money over into my name. Not money, assets. But those assets are no good to me. I could care less about that shit."

Greg climbed back into the car to find Dee Dee still carrying on about corpus delicti and money transfers and Ronald. *Good God almighty,* he thought. He reached up to give Mike's shoulder a squeeze. *Welcome to my world, dude.*

"There's no insurance policy I can promise you," Dee Dee said. "But Abraham doesn't want to be found so I can tell you, if you take the rap, he is not going to show up. He does not want to be found. But I guarantee you, Ronald has killed him. I just know it because the man threatened to kill my son. He called and proved to me he knew my son's number. I just can't find this fucker. If I could find him, I wouldn't be in this situation."

Mike Smith stroked his beard and turned to face Dee Dee head-on. "You need to get with them to find out if this man is dead, if it's true or not," he said sternly. "I got a homeboy that went through this, that did the same thing for somebody."

"Uh-huh. And then what happened?" asked Dee Dee.

"Motherfucker showed up so then they tried to get him for insurance fraud and all this kind of shit, saying he was in cahoots with the guy."

"Ohhhh."

"That's what I'm saying. That insurance shit is a whole different ball game."

Greg sensed that Dee Dee was beginning to cool to the proposition of hiring Mike to take the fall. Her repeated references to Ronald and no mention of the gun plan they had discussed made him worry that she was having second thoughts.

"Why didn't you run?" she asked Mike. "You don't want to run?" As usual, Dee Dee was obsessed with getting away from trouble, not facing it, standing accountable for it, and or making atonement.

"I've been thinking 'bout that too, but hell, eventually I'm gonna fucking go," said Mike. "My boy stepped to me with this here, I said, 'Hell, at least this way I can make a little cash and take care of my fucking boy while I'm gone.'"

"Take care of your what?"

"My boy."

"Oh, you have a family."

"Yeah."

"But see, if I offer Ronald something, I can find out exactly what happened that day, everything they did. And just tell them everything they did and that protects my son."

I've got to save this thing, Greg thought. *She's veering*

*off from the fall-guy plan. Plus, this dude is harping on all
that insurance shit. Damn!*

"Listen, what you do, you call Ronald and you tell
this motherfucker, 'Listen here, we fixing to get you out
of this shit,'" Greg said, barging into the conversation.
"'We need to know where this motherfucker at and if
you done did it, where he at so I can take care of it,'"
Greg instructed her.

"Okay," Dee Dee said demurely.

"You feel me what I'm saying?" Greg continued, reeling Dee Dee back in. "I mean, this one of my partners
that I can trust." He nodded toward Mike.

"Well, then I don't ever have to worry about moving
and changing my name," Dee Dee said, lightly.

"You ain't got to do nothing," Greg said. "Me and
my partner gonna handle this shit. I only got one person
that I can go to like this here and he wouldn't be here if
I couldn't trust him."

Dee Dee riddled Mike with more questions. Would
he change his mind? Wasn't he worried about the Polk
County detectives? Didn't he want to exact revenge on
the people who'd turned him in? How about admitting
to the murder but then hiding out in one of her houses
for the next twenty-five years?

"Shit, that ain't gonna fucking last," Greg interjected.
"You can't be no hermit for twenty-five fucking years."

But Dee Dee persisted. "You can admit it on the
phone," she said. "I'd hide him out for twenty-five years;
why couldn't we? There's people I know in Panama City.
He could live on the beach."

Greg and Mike greeted Dee Dee's absurd proposal with silence. Greg caught Mike shooting him an incredulous *Can you believe this bitch right here*? look through the rearview mirror. Dee Dee seemed oblivious to the men's exasperation, fluffing her hair in the quiet.

"Well, if I find out everything Ronald did and tell him that I've got somebody, that way they don't have to kill my son and have to harass me anymore, I'll fix everything that they've done if he tells me everything they done and where he's at and everything," she said. "And then, what do you want?"

"Fifty grand," Mike said without hesitation.

"Okay," said Dee Dee. "Can I do it in payments? 'Cause I don't have that kind of cash; I'm gonna have to sell something."

"I'm gonna need ten up front," Mike said. "Once I do this, make sure my boy get the money."

"And, see, what I'll do, I'll get it and get it to his mama," Greg added.

"Okay. Well I'm gonna have to sell a house. I'm gonna have to sell that house. That house is gonna sell for thirty-five thousand." Dee Dee seemed to be talking to herself as she mused about selling one of the houses she had foreclosed on after taking over Abraham's outstanding loans, many of them collateralized by homes. Money from the sale of one small house would cover the fall-guy's fee, she said.

"We can do this," Mike said, "but like I said, I'm gonna need a body. Because with a body I can probably get a plea deal with them and make them run the sentences concurrent. They definitely gonna want the fucking body."

"What he's saying, without a body, they gone try to stick him," Greg explained. "If he got a body, he can cut a deal."

"I still need to know how he fuckin' did it," Mike said. "I don't want to go there and say 'I shot the man,' and he show up with his fucking throat cut."

For the next several minutes, Dee Dee recycled her old explanations and excuses as Greg sat in disgust, anxious about getting her back on track. He needed to keep her focused on the agreement they had just reached and on finding out where Abraham was buried. He had no doubt now that Dee Dee knew exactly what had happened to Abraham. He had no doubt that she had either killed him herself or had had him killed. He was just as certain that Abraham was buried on her property somewhere. Dee Dee might think she was fooling everyone else with all the talk about Ronald and fake speculation about what had happened to Abraham, but Greg was a man of the streets. He could decipher bullshit and read between the lines as good as anyone anywhere, anytime.

"You need to get Ronald on the phone tonight," he said, accepting the "Ronald" ruse, careful not to remind the crazy woman that he'd been there when she concocted him.

"Right," said Mike, playing along as well. "If you get with Ronald ass and Ronald can tell us where the fucking body is, I make this fuckin' plea deal, I can tell them the body is right here and they'll go fucking dig him up and then they'll have a body."

"Okay, okay. Deal, okay? All right," Dee Dee said. "Just don't talk to Detective Wallace or Clark."

"They probably definitely gonna come see me," Mike said.

"Yeah, but you don't have to say anything to them."

"I'm gonna have to talk to them or somebody to get this damn deal."

"But the problem is that they're going to try to say, no matter what, they're going to keep bugging [you] until they say that I paid [you] to do it."

"What do I know about you?" Mike said. "All I know is that white girl. What the fuck do I know about you? What do you know about me?"

"Nothing. You should know all kinds of stuff because I'm on the news."

"The shit that's on the news, but what can I tell them about you? Can't tell them a fucking thing about you."

"Okay. Well, let me go get ahold of Ronald then," said Dee Dee, gathering her purse. She and Greg got out of the car.

"Get with Ronald, find out what the fuck we need to know," Mike called out to her as she and Greg began walking away.

"Okay. Thank you. It was nice meeting you," Dee Dee said with a wave of the hand.

Later, Mike said he couldn't help but marvel at her cheerful good-bye.

CHAPTER THIRTEEN

. . . . .

The detectives were elated by what they learned from Dee Dee Moore's meeting with undercover officer Mike Smith. She had not only all but admitted that Abraham Shakespeare was dead, but had intimated that his corpse was buried on her own property. They did worry that Dee Dee might panic once she realized exactly what she'd said to Mike and Greg, and that she might do something to hide essential evidence, so they instructed Greg to suspend his meetings and conversations with Dee Dee for the time being. In the meantime, they would step up their surveillance to see what, if anything, she might do in light of her quasi confessions, particularly what actions she might take on her properties. Accordingly, Greg did not answer any of the several calls Dee Dee made to him on January 24, 2010, and would not call her back until Detective Dave Wallace gave him the green light to contact her.

"We're close, real close," Wallace told Greg. "We got to get her to give us more detail. We need to nail this thing now while she's talking."

"Abraham's body is out there on her property," Greg said with confidence. "I can feel it in my bones. She didn't come right out and say it, but she might as well have said it."

"Could be, but that's why we need to nail her down on this," Wallace reiterated. "You've got to get her to tell you where Abraham is, where his body is."

"Well, you know I'm gonna do all I can to get it out of her."

"If anyone can do it, you can."

"I'll think of something. Right now, I'm gonna call her and set up the next meeting. I'm gonna tell her it's like an emergency."

"Right. And we'll meet first real quick before you hook up with her."

"Okay. I'm gonna call Dee Dee."

Greg placed the call after midnight, apologizing for missing Dee Dee's calls but now insisting that he had an urgent matter to discuss with her.

"There's stuff I've got to tell you," Greg said. "It's important. We got to move."

"What kind of stuff?"

"I gotta tell you face-to-face."

They agreed to meet early the next morning.

"What's wrong with you?" Dee Dee asked as she got into Greg's car in the Lakeland Mall parking lot.

"I was over to some of my partners' house, watching the damn football game last night," Greg began. "Some guys went around talking about this damn case, you know, Shakespeare shit. So, you know, my ears was wide open, not knowing some of these guys work for the Hillsborough Sheriff's Office."

Dee Dee stared at Greg's face, watching him intently.

"I'm listening and they was like, 'Man, these mother-fuckers fixing to release a search warrant for this lady's property.' So I hauled ass out of there, saying I was tipsy or some shit, and then I called you."

He braced himself for what he was sure would be a hysterical reaction to this news. Instead, Dee Dee homed in on the legitimacy of a raid.

"See, how are you gonna issue a search warrant when the parents, when the mother has said she's seen the man?" Once again, Dee Dee was repeating the lie—her lie—that Elizabeth Walker had recently seen her son and told authorities so. Greg had no patience with that.

"The motherfuckers can do anything because they . . ." Greg began.

"Yeah, but Ms. Walker told them, the mother of the son told them she seen the son and signed a sworn affida-vit," said Dee Dee as emphatically as if it were the God's honest truth.

"My first thing was, 'Oh my God, it's time to fuckin' move.'" Greg said, steering the conversation back to his urgent matter. "I wouldn't have called you like that. I called [Mike] and told him, 'Man, come and meet me somewhere.' He said, 'Tell her it's time to move.'"

Again, Dee Dee seemed to ignore the urgency of Greg's news.

"I need to cut a deal with them that they can't touch any of my assets, any of my properties, any of my money if I tell them who I think has done something to Abraham, you know what I mean? I need to have my lawyer work a deal with them," Dee Dee insisted.

"All you got to do is let me handle this shit, 'cause I got some help now," Greg shot back, trying to steer Dee Dee back to the emergency at hand.

What about their plan to get Mike's fingerprints on a gun so he could produce a murder weapon to buttress his confession? Dee Dee asked. And what about the fact that the gun was registered to her?

"What we gonna do is get that bitch and grind all the serial numbers off it," Greg said. "Then we put [Mike's] handprints on it and we put it somewhere."

While Greg focused on what to do with Dee Dee's gun, she continued mumbling about cutting a deal with authorities to protect her bank accounts, houses, cars, furniture, clothing, and jewelry from confiscation.

"I want to make my deal so they can't touch any of my assets," she said. "I know where somebody's at that possibly has something to do with Abraham, because this is the guy who kept calling me. I finally found out who he is. He called himself Ronald but he goes by a different name. Ronald's not his name. Cut a deal where my attorney has to take them a paper where they sign off where they say they won't touch nothing I have, none of my properties, nothing, as long as I tell him who this guy is, you see what I mean?"

Greg tamped down his anger with Dee Dee's fantasies—*enough of this Ronald shit*, he thought—but did not mind showing his impatience. A search warrant was about to be executed, he thundered. They needed to stay focused on getting the gun and removing the body.

"While you trying to cut a deal, we need to be digging," he said forcefully. "It need to be done tonight. We need to get in your truck and you need to take me and ride me and show me the vicinity and you can kind of point in the direction and I'll take it on my own to go where it's at."

Abraham's body might be nine feet below ground, Dee Dee said matter-of-factly. Greg felt his heart rev up. *Who would say how far down a body had been buried unless, first, they knew there was a body and, second, they knew exactly what had been done with it?* He worked to contain his excitement and distract Dee Dee from her own self-incrimination by going over the details of how he planned to retrieve Abraham's remains.

"What's going to have to happen, we're going to have to tie a rope," Greg said. "Is there a tree around? We're going to have to tie a rope around the tree and I'm gonna lower myself down there to get him." He told Dee Dee to get him a twenty-five-foot-long rope. She told him she already had several gallons of bleach on hand to disinfect the ground and cover up or destroy any forensic evidence. But what about any nosy neighbors?

"They ain't gonna be able to see me 'cause I'm going to hit that bitch round six o'clock in the morning," Greg said, assuredly.

"You want to do it tonight?" Dee Dee asked instead. That would work, she said, because her boyfriend's mother, who lived next door to the dig site, was coming over to her house for dinner.

"Tonight'll be great," Greg said, adding that he would get Mike to come out to the burial site and help him. Dee Dee offered her truck and trailer for the operation. If anyone asked, he could say he borrowed them because he was doing some work for her company.

"Park that fuckin' truck right where it's at and you get your ass away from there," he said with authority. "You go home. You go to the fuckin' house. Because if anything happens to us, which I doubt, you won't be no—your alibi you was home and you didn't know, maybe we was trying to plant the bitch there, you understand what I'm saying? We was putting the bitch there to set you up. So, I don't need you there. I need you home at that time."

Greg instructed Dee Dee to make several purchases—a metal trough, more bleach, heavy rope, gloves, and a shovel. Dee Dee was to leave the truck, trailer, and the materials Greg needed behind a house she owned on Highway 60 East in Plant City. After removing the body, Greg and Mike would saturate the ground with bleach and cover their tracks. She was to be at her home in Lakeland, where she and Shar, her young live-in lover, would host a spaghetti dinner for her son, R. J., and Shar's mother, Patricia. Just another easy evening in Lakeland.

Greg could not believe that he might be reaching the end of the long, tricky road he had travelled to get Dee Dee Moore. She still had not said how his old friend had died or at whose hand, but at long last, she had spilled the beans about Abraham's body, and this major break would surely lead to the circumstances and culprits.

Although this woman had almost slipped out of his grip and wasted his efforts with her zigzagging plans, demented schemes, fictitious third parties, and obsession with holding on to the goodies she had collected at Abraham's expense, Greg was pleased with himself for having gotten Dee Dee to entrust him with information that could put this long, tragic mystery to rest and exact some justice from it. As soon as Dee Dee left his sight, he sped off to his prearranged rendezvous point with detectives to give them the damning digital recording.

"Abraham's dead," he said, handing over the recorder. "He's at her house in Plant City. He's buried out back behind the house, about nine foot down."

"You got that on tape?" said Wallace, incredulously.

"All right there on the tape. I'm supposed to go dig him up tonight, me and Mike. Then Mike will supposedly turn himself in, as far as Dee Dee knows. But she wants to cut a deal with the Polk County Sheriff's Office."

"Deal. Yeah, right," said Wallace. "We got a deal for her. Where is she now?"

"She said she was going to get the gun," Greg said. "I'm gonna meet her later and get it. She wants to put Mike's fingerprints on it so he can turn it over as the murder weapon."

"When and where?"

"She's gonna call me and tell me what time and where. But she said she was going to go get the gun now."

"Okay, let us know."

"I'll give you the heads up. Where you want me to meet y'all?"

"Plant City Police Department. Parking lot."

"Okay. I'll call you soon as I know."

"Right," said Wallace. "And, Greg, good work."

Two hours later, Dee Dee sent a text inviting Greg to meet her in thirty minutes at a convenience store parking lot in Plant City. Greg rushed to the Plant City Police Department, where Dave Wallace and Lieutenant Jamie Rudd outfitted him with a fresh digital recorder before he took off for his meeting with Dee Dee.

The big woman plopped into Greg's car and immediately pulled a .38 Smith and Wesson from her pants pocket.

"Listen, you need to take a screwdriver 'cause this is a laser one," she said. "You need the screwdriver to take the battery out. See, watch. You hit that and you hit this button. Laser."

She had been thinking about the body retrieval, Dee

Dee said, and had decided it would be best if Greg and Mike took Abraham's remains out into the countryside to burn it. Greg was horrified by her cold and heartless proposition but knew he could not afford to show it. Not after having gotten this far. With all the evenness he could muster, he deadpanned that if she wanted the body burned, she would need to add kerosene or diesel fuel to her shopping list.

And maybe some marshmallows too, she giggled.

"We gonna take it and once we burn it, we gonna take this shit, put it in a bag and we gonna bury it somewhere else remote," he assured her, swallowing his disgust.

And one other thing, Dee Dee said: be sure to check all over Abraham's body to see if he had any cash on him. She'd heard he had $67,000 on his person when he died. That was more than Greg could agree to, even as part of his act. He would not pillage Abraham's body, he told her, no matter how much money might be in his pockets.

Dee Dee flipped the gun back and forth, peering into crannies for serial numbers. Greg decided to test her familiarity with the gun so he could attest to her handling skills.

"You need to take it apart to see if there's some numbers inside somewhere," he said, eager for her reaction.

Dee Dee began to methodically dismantle the firearm. "Right there," she said, pinpointing serial numbers on two spots on the handgun. "There and there."

"That's it," Greg said. "Those two right there."

"I just want to make sure there's no more hidden, 'cause they could have them internal. You know they can be pretty slick," Dee Dee said, peeking into the gun's nooks. "I could say I sold this to Abraham."

"We're gonna go through this motherfucker," Greg said. "There's only so many places. I'm gonna take all this shit here, all this identification. Anything that identifies this."

"I'd take this whole grip off," Dee Dee said coolly. "Take the whole grip off and take the whole laser system off and keep it. And take the battery out."

She attempted to hand the gun parts to Greg, but he insisted she place them on his lap. "I ain't gonna touch none of this shit," he said. "I don't need none of my fingerprints on this motherfucker."

At one o'clock in the afternoon, Greg pulled into a convenience store in Mulberry to meet the detectives. As he approached their car, cradling the dismantled gun in his shirt, Wallace ran to meet him.

"Here you go," he said. "This the gun Dee Dee gave me. I want you to know now that I never touched it with my bare hands. I made her take it apart so I could see that she knew how the gun worked. And I told her to put it in my lap."

"Got it," said Wallace, carefully lifting the gun parts with his gloved fingers and depositing them in an evidence bag.

"Now here's what's next," Greg said, lighting up a smoke. "She wants me to meet her in another couple of hours and we're supposed to go to the spot on her property in Plant City where Abraham's body is buried."

"She's got two houses out there. Which one is it?"

"I don't know for sure. She's supposed to take me there when I meet up with her. I'll let y'all know where we're meeting soon as I know."

A team of homicide detectives from the Hillsborough County Sheriff's Office pulled up as Greg was preparing to leave. Wallace, Clark, and Lynn briefed them about the gun exchange and about the upcoming trip to the alleged burial site. If Abraham Shakespeare's body was indeed on the property in Plant City, Wallace knew he would be working with the Hillsborough County folks from then on, since the corpse was in their county.

"We need search warrants for two addresses on State Road 60 East and we need 'em in a hurry," Lynn told his befuddled Hillsborough County counterparts.

The Polk County men knew that, although they had worked the case since the beginning—one they could not put down even after the sheriff's office had cut off overtime pay on the case—they would have to yield now to Hillsborough County. It was only natural that Hillsborough would have questions and want some fast answers, and Lynn didn't want to piss them off, but there was no time to waste now.

"It's a really long story, but kind of trust us for now," Lynn said. "We sure would appreciate it if you could get those warrants stat."

Midafternoon on January 25, 2010, Dee Dee wheeled her big white truck and trailer onto State Road 60 and headed east for about eight miles before turning into the driveway of a split-level, wood-frame house near the corner of Farkas Road. She pulled the truck around to the left side of the house, parking it there to obscure any views of the backyard. Having met her in a nearby lot, Greg followed in his Camry.

"I got all the stuff in here," she said to Greg, opening the door of the truck's trailer and rifling through the supplies she had assembled for the dig. Greg took a quick inventory, paying particular attention to the wheel of thick rope among the goods.

"Good, good," he said. "And I see you got plenty of bleach."

Dee Dee scampered over to a spot in the yard and returned with a small piece of iron, which she placed atop a concrete slab in the backyard.

"That's where you should dig," she said, pointing to the angle iron. "Right under there. Maybe six feet down."

Greg no longer felt he had to hide his shock.

"Aw, man, that's where my boy is?" he said, mournfully, staring at the marked spot.

"The drug dealers killed him," Dee Dee said in a near whisper. "They got into it with Abraham in that house next door and that's where they killed him." She knew, she said, because Ronald had finally told her everything and had even provided her with a schematic of where to find the body. She ran to the truck to retrieve a spiral notebook containing a small crude drawing of the concrete slab.

Greg could hardly believe what he was hearing. At last, Dee Dee had stated, unequivocally, that Abraham was dead. She had told him where it happened. She had said how it happened, though Greg knew the "Ronald" story was a cover-up. Had he been alone, he might have danced a jig, such was his excitement. But he knew it was critical now that he keep up the pretense of wanting to help a friend get herself out of a world of trouble.

"So you got everything, right?" Dee Dee said, brushing her hands and turning to leave. "I'll be at my house." She told him that her boyfriend Shar's mother would be arriving for dinner at her house around 6:30 P.M. "So you ought to be good to go after, like, 7:30."

"I'm good," Greg said quietly, still stunned by Dee Dee's matter-of-fact revelations. "I'm gonna go get Mike and we'll get this shit done and cleared after it's dark out here."

Greg felt heavy as he walked back toward the truck. He stopped and turned to look at the concrete slab and the iron bar laid near one corner. According to Dee Dee, his old friend was down there. Abraham was dead, dumped and buried in a backyard, entombed in yards of dirt and a thick blanket of concrete. As relieved as he was to finally have confirmation, it broke Greg's heart to think of it.

"He's at 5802 State Road 60 East in Plant City," Greg said somberly to Wallace and the other detectives at his debriefing later that evening. He handed over Dee Dee's spiral notebook to the detectives.

"Y'all can go get him."

CHAPTER FOURTEEN

·····

While Dee Dee Moore busied herself with dinner guests, Greg bided his time inside his Camry in a mall parking lot, keeping his distance from the swarms of police converging on Abraham Shakespeare's presumed makeshift gravesite.

Around 8:00 P.M., he took a long drag on his cigarette, picked up his phone, and dialed Dee Dee. He and detectives had agreed that luring her away from her home would avoid a scene that Dee Dee's young son might find disturbing.

"Hello?" she said. In those two syllables, Greg could tell that Dee Dee was alarmed to hear from him. He was ready for his scene.

"What the fuck you doing?" he screamed into the phone. "You trying to set me up?"

"What?" she said, nervously. "Greg, what do you mean? What's wrong?"

"I went out to the house out there and there's cops all over the damn place! All kinds of trucks and cars and big lights."

"What?"

"What the fuck is this, Dee Dee? You better not be trying to make me take the rap for this shit, not to mention how this gonna fuck Mike's deal up."

"I would never do that. I would never do that. I don't know any more than you do why they're out there. Who is it, Wallace and Clark?"

"Fuck, I don't know who is out there. Probably Wallace and Clark. All I know is it's a bunch of motherfuckers out there with all this equipment and bright lights and shit, like they know something."

"Oh my God."

"Yeah, oh my God is right. Did you tell somebody else 'bout this shit?"

"Hell no I didn't tell anybody else, Greg. And you know I wouldn't set you up. I don't know what the hell this is. You said they were pulling search warrants . . ."

"Yeah and you should have told me about this shit a long time ago instead of running around in circles and costing us time."

"I know, I know, but I . . ."

"Well, it's a fucked-up situation now."

"Where are you?"

"I'm way down the road from that house. Soon as I seen all that shit going on, we hightailed it out of there."

"I swear to you, Greg, I don't know nothing about this."

"Well, we need to regroup now 'cause this shit just got real. I need you to meet me now."

Dee Dee protested that she had people over.

"I don't give a fuck about all that right now, Dee Dee," said Greg. "Do you get what's going on? The fuckin' police is swarming your property you say Abraham is buried on. Ain't no way I can go in there now. We got a major problem here, babe. Major problem."

"Well, what should we do?"

"Meet me at the mall in fifteen, twenty minutes."

"Okay. Oh my God. Okay."

Dee Dee told everyone that her friend Judy Haggins was having car trouble and was broken down on a dark road somewhere. She had to go help her, she said, but would be back.

At the Hillsborough Sheriff's Office, deputies still were scurrying to obtain search warrants for the two houses on State Road 60 East, the probable murder and burial sites of Abraham Lee Shakespeare.

Dee Dee pulled up to the parking lot and next to Greg's Camry.

"What's going on?" Dee Dee said in a whispery voice as she got into his car, her brow furrowed with worry.

"I don't know what the fuck is going on but your house looks like they're making a SWAT team movie over there," Greg said. "Either they doing that search warrant or somebody tipped 'em off."

"You don't think I told anybody do you? Why in the world would I ever do that?"

"I don't know what to think. I just know . . ."

Greg froze as two cars screeched into the lot, coming to rest in front of his car and Dee Dee's. Detective Dave Wallace stepped out of one, and Detective David Clark stepped out of the other.

"We need both of you to come with us down to the sheriff's office," said Wallace. "Now. You need to follow us to the office."

Dee Dee immediately broke down, sobbing as she pulled out of the lot behind one of the officer's cars. Greg followed in his Camry, talking to himself. *We got you now. This shit is over.*

"You got him!" Dee Dee exclaimed in the interrogation room.

"Got who?" asked Detective Clark.

"You got the guy who killed Abraham. That guy with me, Greg. He killed him."

The detectives looked at each other and shook their heads. They weren't at all surprised by this turn of events. Indeed, they weren't surprised by anything Dee Dee Moore said anymore.

"Now, you know that Greg didn't kill Abraham Shakespeare," Wallace said.

"But he did. He's the one who killed Abraham," Dee Dee insisted through her tears.

"Dee Dee, Greg Smith is working with us," said Clark. "He's been working with us for a while on this case."

Dee Dee froze in her chair and stared at Clark for a moment before taking a long, deep breath.

"Well, then, there's this other guy, his name is Mike, he . . ."

"Dee Dee," Wallace interjected, "are you talking about big, tall Mike with the dreads who you were going to pay to take the fall for killing Abraham? That Mike? I got news for you: he's an undercover detective."

That revelation sent Dee Dee reeling. "Oh my God!" she wailed as her face reddened and tears cascaded down her face. She lay her head on the table and sobbed hysterically.

"Why don't you try telling us the truth, Dee Dee," Clark prodded. "You need to tell the truth, Dee Dee. That you killed Abraham and buried him in your backyard."

"But I didn't!" she shouted. "These drug dealers did it. Yes, it was in my office, but I didn't have anything to do with it."

"So he was killed in your office," said Clark.

The sniveling woman brushed away her tears and unleashed a dizzying set of details.

Abraham had come to the house at 5732 State Road 60 one day in early April 2009 in the company of two or three drug dealers, she said, men she did not know, though she did catch that one of their names was Ronald. When Abraham told her he wanted $200,000 cash to give to the thugs, Dee Dee said, she tried to talk him out of it, but Abraham insisted. She and Abraham argued.

Then an argument broke out among the men, and one of the drug dealers reached into her open gun safe, grabbed her .38 caliber Smith and Wesson, and fired two bullets into Abraham.

The detectives fidgeted as Dee Dee spun her web. Their job required them to listen to this balderdash, but it was hard to just sit still and let someone shower them with pathetic lies.

"Now you know and I know that there is no 'Ronald,'" Wallace said, tired of the charade. "That's a name you made up, or did you forget that?"

Rather than answer directly, Dee Dee clenched her teeth and calmly declared, "I didn't kill the man."

"Then who did? Who did?" Wallace shouted. "Who did it? Who killed him?"

"I can't tell you."

"Why, Dee Dee? Why can't you tell me?"

Dee Dee rubbed her brow and scrunched her face as if it pained her to think.

"Okay. He was caught with forty kilos of cocaine," she said, "and the guy's name is . . . It was a drug deal that went bad. It was a drug deal that went bad, and the guy's name is, um, um, some . . . I just found it out today or yesterday. It's, um, I'm trying to think of his name. He just . . . He just went down for it. It's . . . I have it written down at home. I'm trying to think of the guy's name." She paused, then said, "Why can't you just arrest me?"

"You can't tell us because it's you and you're scared," Clark claimed.

"Why would I say arrest me then and charge me with it?" she said to Clark.

"Who's so important that you're going to take the charge?" Clark asked, leaning back in his chair. "Let's hear this whopper."

Dee Dee paused and looked at Wallace. "You know I didn't kill him," she said.

"No, I don't. I do not know this," Wallace said angrily. "Don't you say that. I do not know this."

"Dee Dee," Clark said, counting off the evidence. "The recordings, everything. The individual, Greg, that you sat there and pointed out where the frickin' body is on your property. Once this is laid out in front of a jury, you know what they're going to be doing?"

Dee Dee sniveled and shook her head.

"Who shot Abraham?" Wallace interjected.

"You know who shot him," Dee Dee said.

Weary of the farce and getting nowhere, the detectives tried once more to get a straight answer out of Dee Dee. This time, she had a question for them.

"If I tell you the truth about who killed Abraham," she asked breathlessly, "can I keep my things?"

Without a confession and, as yet, no body, detectives let Dee Dee go home that night, warning her not to leave the area and to expect to hear from them again. Greg went home too, turning over his trusty tape recorder to the detectives for the last time.

CHAPTER FIFTEEN

.....

Responding to the detectives' request for another interview the next day, January 25, Dee Dee again identified the murder scene as the one-story, redbrick, ranch-style house at 5732 State Road 60 East, the house she had been renting for her medical staffing business since 2008 and where her boyfriend's mother lived in exchange for her work with Dee Dee's company. Briefly, Dee Dee's attorney friend Howard Stitzel had set up an office there too, but once renovations were completed on the house next door—the split-level at 5802 State Road 60 East that Dee Dee also owned—Stitzel moved his law office there.

Dee Dee told detectives that Abraham was buried beneath a thirty-by-thirty-foot concrete slab in the backyard of 5802. She admitted that she had bought lime to cover Abraham's body.

As Dee Dee was being questioned, deputies had been

busy executing search warrants for both residences. Early on the morning of January 26, 2010, droves of investigators, including an anthropologist from the University of Southern Florida, finally descended on the properties where Abraham Shakespeare had met his dreadful end. Sheriffs' department helicopters swam the skies overhead, surveying the panorama.

Armed with trowels, shovels, scoops, soil sifters, metal detectors, and cameras, the team foraged the front yards and backyards for clues and evidence, collecting any scraps that might be telling—pieces of plastic and cloth, soil samples, mops, a beer bottle, and a piece of angle iron among the items that would be marked as evidence. Inside 5732, detectives and technicians tested for blood on the floors, the walls, appliances, and furniture. They shaved a section of carpet near the kitchen door where a swab of phenolphthalein had yielded a positive reading for blood. Other detectives scattered across the house, gathering files, photographs, computer disks, hard drives, flash drives, DVDs, CDs, and bank statements—anything that might help show the trail of activity that established a motive behind Abraham's tragic demise. Heavy excavation equipment and its operators stood at the ready next door at 5802, where the concrete slab lay.

Another team of investigators fanned out across Hillsborough and Polk counties to gather videotapes of Dee Dee's trips to Sam's Club, where she had purchased the items that Greg had ordered for his ostensible exhumation of Abraham's remains; to find the backhoe that had been used to dig the makeshift grave; and to locate the cement contractor who had poured the concrete slab almost a year earlier.

Yet another team of detectives began calling in witnesses, including lawyer Howard Stitzel and Cedric Edom, the cousin who had filed Abraham's missing-person's report two and a half months earlier.

From his own attorney's office, Howard Stitzel told officers that he had temporarily set up his practice at the 5732 address while waiting for renovations to be completed on what was to be a permanent office space next door, saying he moved into 5802 State Road around mid-June 2009. He admitted that he had created some business documents for Abraham at Dee Dee's request, some of which Abraham had signed in his presence, most notably the assignment of power of attorney to Judy Haggins. As best as he could recall, he had not laid eyes on the man since last April.

But hadn't Howard claimed to have spoken to Abraham by phone in October 2009, in connection with Sentorria Butler's child-support case? Yes, Howard said, but after thinking about it, he could now only say that he *thought* it was Abraham. Dee Dee had handed him the phone that day, saying Abraham was on the line, and he assumed it was so, Howard told the detectives.

That afternoon, Detectives Dave Wallace and Greg Thomas arrived at the Lakeland home of Cedric Edom, who surprised them by producing several digital recordings of conversations with Dee Dee Moore in which she rehashed various accounts of Abraham's whereabouts and the reasons he had left town. What's more, Dee Dee could be heard on the recordings trying to coax Cedric into volunteering another lie to police: that he had seen his cousin attack and choke her and threaten to kill her, wrap her in carpet, and dump her in the lake. In exchange for that testimony, Dee Dee had offered to retire Cedric's debts and give him the deed to his house. Having made the recordings to protect himself against Dee Dee's serial lies, Cedric willingly surrendered the tape recorder to the detectives, along with a cell phone containing several text messages all purportedly sent to him by his illiterate cousin.

As the detectives turned to leave, Cedric handed over one more piece of potential evidence—a drafted affidavit that he said Dee Dee had asked him to sign a couple of weeks earlier. It attested that, about a week after he filed the missing-person's report on his cousin in November, Cedric got a visit from Abraham, who came over to explain why he was going underground. That was not true, said Cedric, so he never signed the affidavit.

In the last days of January 2010, investigators conducted a flurry of interviews, speaking in person or by phone to Dee Dee's associates, former employees, bankers, real-estate agents, lawyers, paralegals, contractors, and handymen. When authorities talked with Judy Haggins on January 27, she told them Dee Dee had called her in the wee hours of the previous day to announce that drug dealers had killed Abraham. According to Judy, Dee Dee said that she, Abraham, Cedric, and Ronald had been arguing over $200,000 when suddenly Abraham put a gun to her head, and she'd passed out in fright. She then came to just in time to see Ronald shoot Abraham and threaten to kill her son if she told anyone.

Back on State Road 60, investigators continued the grueling, painstaking work of sifting through clumps of earth for possible evidence and swabbing surfaces throughout both houses for fingerprints, blood droppings, and other DNA material. Local media, held at bay by yards and yards of yellow crime tape and protective officers, had set up camp along the busy highway, relying on telephoto lenses to capture the cadre of investigators at work behind the neighboring houses. A county excavator had broken up the thick slab of concrete behind the house, and detectives were digging through a three-foot trench by hand, depositing clumps of dirt via a bucket brigade, which passed the soil along five gallons at a time. Shake-screen operators plucked out everything that could possibly be of evidentiary value, no matter how insignificant it might appear.

Shortly after 5:00 P.M. on January 28, after two days of meticulous digging and sifting, the dogged, muddied, and exhausted investigators reached what appeared to be mummified human remains about six feet down. A figure, dressed in a black jacket over a light-colored shirt, purplish denim jeans over boxer shorts, wearing a black belt and black socks but no shoes, was positioned on its left side, a head of long, thick hair gathered in a stocking cap, lain on a bloodstained towel. The metal buttons on the jacket, metal buckle on the belt, and metal zipper on the jeans had been cut away. Most of the body was caked in a hardened white substance, up to six inches thick in some areas, which officials gingerly chipped away.

Hillsborough County sheriff David Gee broke the news to reporters. "It's clearly a human body," he said. "I'll allow the medical examiner to do their investigation and we'll have the body at the medical examiner's office sometime during the night."

Polk County sheriff Grady Judd, standing with Gee, told the media, "During the very beginning of the investigation, what we explained was, we hoped that we would find Abraham alive and well and that he had truly wanted to hide from those that were asking him for money. . . . However, as our investigation continued, the information that we were developing led us to believe that he might very well have ended up with an untimely death by sinister means and motives. Once again, the investigation of the missing person goes on."

As darkness fell, a white van pulled out of the driveway at the split-level house and turned onto State Road 60, transporting the remains to the medical examiner's office. Fingerprint comparisons soon positively identified them as those of Abraham Lee Shakespeare. For the first time in nearly ten months, people knew exactly where he was.

"The body is that of a partially mummified, decomposing, and focally skeletonized man," the medical examiner wrote in his postmortem report the next day. "The skin and muscles on the right side of the face are absent down to the level of the bone. The skin on the left side of the face is absent exposing the left masseter muscle. The nose is absent. The lips are absent. The skin of the neck is preserved and is dark brown with skin slippage along the posterolateral left side of the neck. The skin and muscle of the left shoulder are absent exposing the underling shoulder joint and tendons. The upper extremities are covered by brown, leathery, slightly moist skin with drying of the hands, most prominent on the left. The external genitalia are dried and shrunken. The skin of the back is moist, soft and brown on the left, and leathery and brown on the right."

The medical examiner removed two bullets from the body. One had entered the right upper chest and turned downward. The other had pierced the right lower chest and travelled upward once inside. It had fractured a rib, grazed the aorta, and perforated the right lung.

As expected, the manner of death was designated as homicidal violence. Cause of death: gunshot.

CHAPTER SIXTEEN

•••••

The news about the recovery on State Road 60 spread quickly. Notwithstanding the sheriffs' disclaimer that they couldn't yet say whose remains they had found, no one doubted whose they were. Earlier that day, Detective Clark had driven over to Florida Southern College in Lakeland to break the news to Abraham's mother, who was working in the cafeteria. He pulled her aside and sat her down.

"Look, I can't tell you that we have your son, but we're 99 percent sure that it's your son," he said, somberly explaining what investigators had found. The frail woman buried her face in her hands and cried. Clark put his arms around her. He knew she had tried to prepare herself for this moment, but still . . .

"We're going to get you home, alright?" Clark said. "We're taking care of everything with your supervisors, and they completely understand, so you're going to go home now, okay?" The bereaved woman nodded. A friend had been summoned to take Mrs. Walker back to her little house, and she assured Clark that she would take care of her.

"Poor, poor, sweet lady," Clark whispered as the two women drove off.

That evening, Abraham's mother, brother, and sisters wept, comforting one another in the wake of the shocking, though unsurprising, development. Friends called for justice and vowed to see it done. Antoinette Andrews and Torrie Butler held their children tightly.

"The past few months have been filled with uncertainty and worry over the fate and whereabouts of my son," read a statement released to the media by Elizabeth Walker later that evening. "We had certainly hoped for a different outcome. They didn't care anything about him."

Dee Dee Moore spent the night texting Detective Wallace, telling him that she wanted to talk some more, that she wanted to "tell the truth." In one text, she asserted that "James would not have done this ever," apparently aware that detectives had contacted her ex-husband, James Moore, earlier that evening. Wallace arranged for Dee Dee to come into the Hillsborough County Sheriff's Office the next afternoon to tell her new "truth."

"It's the bottom of the ninth and you've got two strikes, Dee Dee, okay?" Wallace said, his patience wearing thin. "Who killed Abraham, Dee Dee? What's the name?"

"It was a drug deal that went bad and the guy's name is, um, um, something, ah, I just found it out."

Wallace stood back from the table and shouted that he was tired of her lies and her changing stories. "You don't know the guy's name because there was no drug deal," he exclaimed.

"I watched Cedric shoot him. I was in the room," Dee Dee said.

"Oh, now it's Cedric. . . ."

"I'm telling you, Cedric took the gun and cold-blooded, did not hesitate to shoot the man and I seen it happen."

The detectives had long ago come to the conclusion that the woman sitting before them was an inveterate, shameless liar. Still, they were taken aback when, without skipping a beat, she put forth yet another version, beginning once again with Abraham showing up at her office one day with drug dealers in tow. This time, however, Dee Dee didn't portray the argument as having been between Abraham and the dealers but between Abraham and her. She said that when she resisted Abraham's request for $200,000 to hand over to criminals, he grew increasingly agitated. As his fury peaked, she said, Abraham leaped at her, gripped her throat, and began choking her, his face a portrait of rage. Someone shot him, but she wasn't sure who because she was lapsing in and out of consciousness. Maybe she had shot him herself, but in self-defense, she allowed.

Exasperated, the detectives informed Dee Dee that she was playing with fire. Her crazy, ever-changing accounts made no sense and were obvious lies, they said. They were going to find out the truth eventually. Her clumsy attempts at cover-up would only hurt her.

"R. J. shot him," she blurted out, leaving the two hardened detectives frozen in disbelief. "My son, R. J., shot Abraham twice. Abraham was trying to choke me. R. J. walked in the room and grabbed my gun and shot him. He was only protecting me as any son would do."

Both investigators had dealt with plenty of lowlifes before, had heard all kinds of alibis and insane lies, had seen desperate ploys. But a mother blaming her own teenage son for a man's murder? That was a stunner, even coming from Dee Dee Moore.

"Really, Dee Dee?" Wallace said. "You really going to point the finger at your own boy, your own child? You want to us to believe that R. J. killed Abraham Shakespeare. That's your story."

It was, Dee Dee said, and she would not recant it.

"Go home, Dee Dee," Wallace said.

Once Dee Dee left, the detectives looked at each other knowingly. Even though they realized the R. J.–did–it version was bound to be another story concocted out of whole cloth, they would have to speak to the boy if they could. So at 5:30 P.M. that evening, Dee Dee's ex-husband, James Moore, walked into the Hillsborough County Sheriff's Office with ninth-grader Robert James "R. J." Moore, and gave the cops permission to privately interview his underage son.

R. J. told the investigators that he had only seen Abraham Shakespeare twice in his life—once at his family's home and once at the Hard Rock casino. He had heard that people were looking for Abraham, he said, but his mother had always maintained that she didn't know where he was. She had also told him that a guy named Cedric was going around saying she had murdered Abraham. He didn't believe his mother had killed the man, he said.

"Did you kill Abraham Shakespeare, R.J?" the detectives asked.

"No," he said. "I didn't shoot him."

"You didn't see Abraham choking your mother and then shoot Abraham to save your mother?"

If that had happened, R. J. said, he would have called the police.

"So, you didn't shoot Abraham Shakespeare for any reason?" Wallace asked.

"That 100 percent didn't happen," R. J. said.

The following afternoon, Dee Dee began texting Dave Wallace again to request yet another meeting with investigators. Wallace and Hillsborough County Detective Greg Thomas again ushered her into the interview room and again urged her to tell the truth about the shooting and burial.

It was not to be. As they feared, Dee Dee had a new story to tell, at least partly new. The scene was still at 5732 State Road 60, but Dee Dee now recalled that two white men she didn't know—again drug dealers, she claimed—had shown up in her office where Abraham was visiting on April 6, 2009, and an argument had quickly ensued. Abraham, she said, had pulled out a gun and fired it at Howard Stitzel, Dee Dee's lawyer and office-mate. But the gun didn't go off, she said, so Howard had grabbed her .38 Smith and Wesson from an open safe and shot Abraham twice in the chest. Howard then left with one of the unnamed men, and the other drug dealer stayed behind to arrange for disposal of Abraham's body. All Dee Dee had to do was have a hole dug outside.

The new tale did not begin to pass muster with the detectives, and they let Dee Dee know it in no uncertain terms. She in turn complained that the detectives weren't looking into any of the suspects she was giving them.

"Dee Dee, why do I need to go in circles when the person that can answer the question is sitting right in front of me? The one person who's got a dead body in their backyard, who's got all the money of the dead guy, who's got all the knowledge is right here and then you're telling me to run around and talk to everybody else? You knew that he didn't have shoes on. Come on."

"Because I was told that," she whimpered.

"You lie profusely," Wallace said pointedly.

"You're blackmailing me to give you a name."

Detective Thomas piped up. "You're the person who killed Abraham and buried him," he said, letting it sink in for a minute. "I think tomorrow we're gonna get a phone call about ten o'clock in the morning, you know, 'Guys, I really want to come in and tell you the truth.'"

"You should know why I can't tell you."

"Why can't you tell me, Dee Dee? Oh, 'cause you don't know his name? Who killed the man? If you didn't do it, Dee Dee, who did it? How does a thirty-seven-year-old white woman from Plant City end up in this predicament? This is silly. And you're sitting there acting like a complete idiot. 'I can't, I can't, I can't.'"

"You know I didn't kill him."

"No, I don't know that. I don't know that. Don't sit there and say I know that. I don't know that. I know that you have lied and lied profusely, that's what I know."

"I have had to lie profusely because you don't believe me, you don't believe me."

"I don't believe you because they're lies. How can I believe lies? You've lied because I don't believe you. That makes no absolute sense at all. I didn't believe you because they were lies. Okay. My God, I didn't believe lies. So I guess if I'd believed your first lie then you wouldn't have to lie any more, right?"

Wallace paced the floor, exasperated.

"I guess it's so important that you can't tell us that you're going to let your son go without his mother for the rest of his life," he said. "Dee Dee, you don't realize that we're talking about life in prison here? We're talking about the rest of your life. We're talking about a potential death penalty case."

"That's not fair."

"At the very least, you are part of accessory to murder. At the very, very least."

Silence swallowed the room. Dee Dee sat in a chair against the wall with her legs and arms crossed, shaking her head. Like every other time, she had given the detectives only more questions, not answers, and more detours than leads. But they were unmoved in their belief that Abraham Shakespeare's killer was sitting in front of them.

* * *

After nearly a week of interviewing witnesses, assisting at the crime scene, and tracking down leads, leaving no stone unturned, detectives were barraged by unsolicited tips, most of them from anonymous callers. Some tips had actually been helpful, like the phone call that came in from Dee Dee's brother, who said his parents had some information that might be useful to the investigation and wanted to talk. He said his sister was trying to get their elderly, ailing father to take the rap for Abraham's murder.

On the evening of January 30, Polk County detective Dave Wallace and Hillsborough County detective Preston Hollis headed out to Linda and Patrick Donegan's trailer on Turkey Creek Road, where Detective Hollis settled in one room with Dee Dee's father, and Detective Wallace met with Mrs. Donegan in another.

"We went over to see how she was," Patrick said, explaining that he and his wife had visited their daughter the night before. "We took her some ABC pizza and a salad she likes. And then we'd all be sitting down talking and she's telling us, you know, things like 'They think R. J. did it' and all this stuff. And I said, 'Well, I wished I could just take all of it for ya,' you know?"

"Meaning you wanted to take the burden off your daughter?" Hollis asked.

"Yeah, off my daughter. And, uh, she said, 'Well, would you, Dad?' And then I didn't speak too much about it."

Hollis studied the old man's weary face.

"She comes over here this morning and she was sitting here and I said, you know, 'You all right, kid?'" Patrick continued. "And she said, 'You really would do something like that, Dad?'"

"Meaning would you, that you would take her place?" Hollis inquired.

"Yeah. It's just a father or daughter or whatever. You know how your kids get sick, I really wished I could have this."

"Right."

"So, I ain't said much to her about it. And she said, 'Well, you're old, getting old' and all this stuff, you know. But that was about all my conversation was."

"Okay. So basically she was just asking if, if you would take her place in all this."

"Basically."

That established, Hollis moved on to another piece of business at hand. He'd heard that Dee Dee had stashed the possible murder weapon at her parents' house. Was that true?

Patrick confirmed that his daughter had brought over three guns to store at the house a while back. One of them was a .38 Smith and Wesson, which she had retrieved a few days ago.

Meanwhile, Linda Donegan was revealing herself to Wallace as a mother who loved her daughter but who had serious doubts about her child's honesty. The night before, Linda said, she'd asked her daughter why she hadn't gone to the police when Abraham was killed and buried.

"She says, "'Cause I was afeared for R. J.'s life that he

was gonna get killed,'" Linda recalled. "'Because what happened that night was Abraham was strangling me 'cause I wouldn't take the amount of money out of the safe that he wanted to give these drug dealers.' So one of 'em, when Abraham started strangling her, uh, shot him in the shoulder here. Then she said, after they took his body out, this guy says that 'don't worry, he's alive.' I said, 'Well then how, if he was alive, why was he digging the hole?' She said, 'Well, uh,' and then she went blank like she's staring into space. Went blank. So right then I knew something was wrong so I decided I'd call y'all today and turn over everything that she gave me to hold 'cause she wanted us to hold her jewelry and cameras and stuff because she said that, uh, drug dealers might wanna steal from her safe up there in Lakeland."

Earlier in the week, Linda said, Dee Dee had come by to borrow a white truck with a hitched trailer.

"So when she left, she was driving the white truck with the trailer," Wallace said.

"Right."

"And she never did tell me why she parked the truck and trailer right there and threw all her brother's stuff out of the trailer into the two-story garage."

"Right."

"Your daughter's name was brought up probably within the last month as a person of interest," Wallace said, shifting gears. "Prior to that did you have any information . . . Had she talked to you anything about Abraham Shakespeare being missing and that the police were talking to her or did you learn about it from the media?"

"She told me that y'all were questioning because Cedric went over there and told them that he was missing since April because Cedric didn't wanna pay for his house he was in, she was trying to collect Cedric's money that she said was owed to Abraham for the house that he lived in, that he had turned . . . Well, it was really owed to her because he'd turned all his assets over to her. And she said Cedric said that he was missing and she said he wasn't missing, he was in, uh, Puerto Rico."

"Oh, she told you [Abraham] was in Puerto Rico?"

"Yes. She told me he was in Puerto Rico one time and then one time she told me he was in Orlando in a hospital but he didn't wanna call and tell his mom 'cause he looked so bad."

"And then now in the last week, since we have found the remains of Abraham Shakespeare on [Dee Dee's] property, what has she told you since that point?"

"Well she told me two different stories. The first story was that three men come up with Abraham and Abraham wanted her to get some money out of the safe for these drug dealers and she said she wasn't gonna get that much money out of the safe and he started to strangle her, so one of these guys shot him in the shoulder and then they dragged him out and they said, 'Oh, don't worry, uh, Miss Moore; he's alive, don't worry.' And then the next story she told me was that, uh, let's see, uh . . . There were two men there and it was a robbery and they shot Abraham," Linda recounted.

"So the first story, I guess, these drug dealers—these robbing, murderous drug dealers—defended her because she was getting strangled by one of the people who was trying to rob her." Wallace chuckled derisively. He couldn't hide his scorn for the web of lies Dee Dee had spun.

What about her daughter's sudden burst of riches? he asked. Did the family ever question Dee Dee about the houses, the trips, the expensive vehicles, the jewelry? Where did she get that kind of money?

"First, it was her veterans' hospital business," said Linda. "I knew she took in a lotta money when she did a lotta jobs, but lately she hadn't been paying attention, she hired somebody else to work the phones and I wouldn't think she's taking in that much money. And then she said she had it all saved up. And then she had money from Abraham giving her 10 percent of a million dollars. And she had money for turning somebody in. 'Cause I asked her how she got the two-story. She said that was from turning somebody in for tax evasion, the two-story and the Corvette. And I don't think the government's gonna pay you that much money."

Wallace laughed aloud at Linda's wry observation. "From what we've seen," he said, "it's been one thing after another all the way back to the Mexicans sexually assaulting her," Wallace said, appreciating Linda's laid-back, salt-of-the-earth demeanor and her willingness to talk about her daughter so frankly.

"Yeah and I didn't even know until I read the newspaper that she's on probation," Linda said. "She had told us three Mexicans stole the car and they didn't appear in court so all the charges were dropped against her, that they ran back to Mexico 'cause they know they were guilty."

"Oh."

"And we were both, now this I don't know if you know, we were both fired from Arcadia Medical business in Tampa."

"I had heard something about . . . I didn't know you were involved in that."

"Well, I didn't know I was involved in it until later I was helping her clear some packages out and I found the slip saying I was fired for, uh, misappropriating funds and I didn't know I was fired for that. I thought they just must've let me go because the office wasn't doing any business and we couldn't get any phone service there."

"Uh-huh."

"The office on the right side had burnt down and, uh, we had moved over to the left side. But then I found out later that [Dee Dee] was paying a lotta people checks before they turned their time slips in. When you're working for a nursing home or hospital, you gotta turn your time slip in first."

"I've talked to some people about that incident and I don't know the whole extent of it, but basically that company said she was misappropriating funds. And I believe they actually talked to the tune of somewhere around $80,000," Wallace told Linda.

"Wow," said Linda. "I knew nothing about that."

"And in fact, according to them, they suspected that the fire may have had to do with Dee Dee."

"I didn't know nothing about that."

Wallace turned his attention to the goods the Donegans were handing over to the detectives. "There's several items here that you're actually turning over to the Hillsborough County Sheriff's Office," he noted. "And these are items that were given to you by your daughter."

"Right, to hold because she said she might need to sell 'em because you all were gonna arrest her for Abraham being missing without even finding the body."

Wallace rummaged through the package of goods, reaffirming the contents with Linda.

"And just to be clear, everything you've turned over to us and all the statements you've given, those have been of your own free will. We haven't coerced you or threatened you or anything like that," he said.

"No, those have been with my own free will, yes."

"Is there anything that we haven't asked you about that you think is important to this investigation or anything else that seems strange to you?"

"No," said Linda. "Just the fact that she was hiding the gun and I think she's been acting funny lately. Very erratic behavior. And she can't seem to answer a question I asked her directly. Starts looking at the sky and out in space. Said she wouldn't tell me why she put my truck and trailer over there."

The detectives could not help but feel sorry for Dee Dee's parents, so obviously worn and wearied by the accumulation of worries and complications visited upon them by a daughter who it seemed they were no longer inclined to defend.

CHAPTER SEVENTEEN

......

After her interview at the Hillsborough County Sheriff's Office on January 30, 2010, Dee Dee Moore stopped texting Dave Wallace and making calls to investigators to request meetings. She had gotten a lawyer, and he forbade her to initiate further contact with authorities.

If the attorney had advised his troubled client to remain silent with all inquirers, however, it was not counsel that Dee Dee took to heart. On February 2, as she pulled out of the driveway on Redhawk Bend Drive, she rolled down her car window, inviting questions from the gaggle of reporters congregated in front of her house.

"What are the circumstances behind [Abraham Shakespeare's] murder?" one asked.

"I can't discuss that. The sheriff's department is working on that."

"But you know, Dee Dee?"

"I have to worry and protect my family and my friends."

"You're implying that you're scared, that somebody might get you?"

"I am. It is very emotional for me. Very emotional. And if anybody would ever endure what I have endured, they would not even begin to understand. Everybody acts differently in every situation. So I'm trying to keep a straight face so that I can talk to you and not act like a crybaby, but I know there are a lot of circumstances behind this and there's a lot of questions to be answered and they will be answered."

"Do you understand how people would think you're guilty?"

"Oh, absolutely, without a doubt. But the people that know me, the people that love me, the people that care about me, and the people that I have talked with, the people that I've been friends with, and the people that know me all my life, would know I would never, ever, ever hurt anybody. That's why I haven't left. I'm not running anywhere. I'm not scared. I'm not scared of going to jail for murder because there is no jury that's going to convict me."

Suddenly, Dee Dee's confident, matter-of-fact tone dissolved into a quivering, stammering whine.

"They're saying that I took a gun, put it up and killed another human being and I would never, ever, ever do that." Then, just as abruptly, Dee Dee the Undaunted returned. "So, no, I don't think any jury would ever convict me of that. I would never take a gun. That is what you're saying. And you're saying that when you do that, you're taking away someone's whole entire life. That means no son, no family, no money in the whole entire world is worth any of that. And that is what is really hard for me to understand that people can't comprehend. I didn't run, I have nothing to hide from. I feel very confident that, if they do that, I will win that case."

Dee Dee punted questions about suspicious text messages purportedly from Abraham, about when he had died, about who or what she was afraid of and other particulars, deferring to the investigation or her lawyer's admonitions. She pounced, however, when a journalist asked how the ordeal had been for her.

"To me, I'm more concerned about my family," she said. "I'm more concerned about my friends. Everybody, you know, all over the state, everybody I know have contacted me and, you know, they know what kind of person I am. So I'm pretty sure with my personality and everything, people know who I am as a person and know what I would do and what I wouldn't do. But everybody has something they get scared of in life. Everybody has that one tragedy. And then they feel bad. And everybody feels bad at some point and don't know what decision to make when they're scared." The tears started to flow again. "So, to that I say, let the courts be the judge of that, let the investigators do their job and they'll bring justice to the right person."

"What do you want the public to know about you?" came the question.

"They know with any police investigation, with anything with the media, they know that everything gets twisted. They know that people add comments. They know that things are not said exactly the way they were put out because it's not fun, it's not good, it's not news. You always want the drama, you want the twist, you want the, you always go to have a good comment with the bad. And that's always, all through life, just like our accolades in life, anything that we've ever done, that's what happens with everybody. You put down someone's comments and then you have to add all the negative behind them. Like, who has records? We have police records of everybody, but do you ever get a record of everything you did good in your life, everything that you've done for other people, every person you've helped? You don't do that. Nobody does. But that's the thing that we need to change in the world and we would have a better place to live in."

Returning to the original pretext for Dee Dee's involvement with Abraham Shakespeare, a reporter asked if Dee Dee was still planning to write a book about the experience.

Yes, she said. "I'm writing what he wanted in there. Like he grew up in the orange field as a child working. And a lot about his family and how he grew up, the way he grew up, and then how money changed his entire life." She already had eight chapters under her belt, she said.

"How does the story end?" asked a shrewd journalist.

"Sadly, now," Dee Dee said.

"Does the story end with an arrest?" the reporter pressed. "Does it end with someone going to jail? How does it end?"

"Well, that's why we have laws and that's why we have investigators," Dee Dee answered. "If they choose to arrest me, then I will have to pay those consequences. I will go to court and fight for my rights because I would never pull a gun on another human being in my life. And the people that know me know I wouldn't do that. So I'm not worried about that."

"Tell us who to focus the attention on," someone said, prompting Dee Dee to wax self-righteous.

"What you need to focus on is giving his family a week to grieve," she said. "He's getting buried on Saturday. Don't any of you have any hearts? Don't any of you think about his family? It shouldn't be about me, it should be about him. A man has died and he's finally getting a proper funeral. He did not deserve to be buried in a backyard like a piece of trash. He did not deserve to be buried in a backyard like a piece of garbage. He deserves a proper funeral, he deserves all his family and friends there. No, the focus should not be on me. The focus should be on his family."

Undeterred by the scolding, a reporter informed Dee Dee that the spotlight had not been aimed at her without reason. For nearly a month, she has been an officially designated "person of interest" in Abraham Shakespeare's disappearance, so of course reporters were interested in her. That reminder then triggered a diatribe about a justice system gone wrong. And another round of Dee Dee's self-absorption.

"Look at all of the people we have arrested innocently during our time," Dee Dee said. "Look at the man that just got out after DNA testing. How many people now have been convicted of a crime they did not do because of DNA evidence? God up above knows I didn't shoot that man and that is the only person I have to answer to. And God knows I would never take another human being's life. So if I can live with that, I can live with anything. No one has to believe me. With the situation the way it went down, I wouldn't believe myself. I'd say, 'Lock her up.' I would. We always know that there's always more to the story, more to the circumstance, more to what we're just seeing. A lot of us just like to look in the box and sometimes you gotta look all the way around the box. I know what's in my heart. I know what kind of person I am and my friends and family knows what kind of person I am and that's all that counts to me. So if I can live with that and walk, and get up every day and survive, I'm not going to start being a drone and hibernate because of all of this. Abraham wouldn't even want that for me. Abraham knew what kind of life he had. He knew how hard it was with the kind of life he had. And money always brings all kinds of people around you and it's sad and it brings a lot of the bad people and a lot of wrong people around you. And to that, I know what I've done and I feel confident and I know what I've done. And I'm confident that whoever decides to make this decision, that they're making a decision on another person's life. A decision that takes a person away from their family for life. And if they can do that with the confidence that they know I definitely did it, then, it's a sad world."

It was irony bordering on the absurd that Dee Dee Moore, of all people, would wax philosophical about money's magnetic appeal to "bad people" and "wrong people." Reporters scribbled madly to keep up with their rambling subject and her treasury of incredible quotes.

After twenty minutes of back and forth, Dee Dee told reporters she had to go and only wished she could discuss more of the case with them. Just before she drove off, she announced that she had no regrets about having met Abraham but wished that she had handled things differently.

"If I would have never helped him out with the financials and everything he asked me to do there, I wouldn't even be looked at or questioned by the sheriff's department," she said. "I never would have gotten involved in all of this."

That very afternoon, as the local television stations prepared their reports of Dee Dee's eccentric curbside press conference for the evening newscasts, Hillsborough County officials were putting the last touches on an arrest warrant for Dee Dee Moore, including a lengthy probable-cause affidavit enumerating her dubious financial transactions, summarizing the multiple twists and turns that marked the search for Abraham, and recapitulating the discovery and retrieval of Abraham's remains. At 5:06 P.M., Hillsborough County deputy Jeramy Manis flashed his police lights at a silver pickup truck and pulled Dee Dee over on a Plant City thoroughfare. Two Hillsborough detectives advised her that she was under arrest, secured her wrists behind her back with handcuffs, pronounced her rights, and led her to the backseat of Manis's patrol car.

"I would have turned myself in," Dee Dee said to Manis

as they drove toward the criminal-investigation division's office. "I came to the office every time I was asked. I'm not going anywhere. I didn't kill anyone. I'm innocent."

Manis had not asked Dee Dee anything. Nor did he respond to her repeated protests of innocence. Only when she asked him to cuff her hands in front of her instead of behind her did he finally speak up, informing her that department policy would not allow that accommodation. Once arrived at central booking, Dee Dee learned that she was being charged with accessory after the fact of first-degree murder. Turning again to Manis, she asked the deputy what kind of sentence the charge carried. "I told her that was up to the judge," Manis wrote in his report. Searched, fingerprinted, and photographed, Dee Dee Moore was placed in an interview room for yet another talk with detectives. Only this time, she was not free to come and go as she chose but, rather, charged under Florida Statute 777.03, which applies to anyone other than a member of the immediate family who helps someone plan or commit a serious crime or helps an offender try to get away with it.

"This investigation is still unfolding right now and I would expect there would be other charges that will be brought by the state attorney," Hillsborough County sheriff David Gee said in a news conference that evening. "Right now this is what we're comfortable with at this point." But yes, he said, Dee Dee Moore could later be charged with murder.

"I won't say that we've identified all of the players involved. I think that we have a good grasp of what's going on," Gee explained. "We are going to find out everybody that was involved. I assure you, it started tonight and Sheriff Judd will tell you the same thing: we are going to seek justice for [Abraham Shakespeare]. And we will find out all of the players, whether they were involved directly in the murder or in the theft of his lottery winnings, we will get to all those things."

The next morning, Dorice Donegan Moore, a week shy of her thirty-eighth birthday, sat among a sea of orange-jumpsuit-clad men and women in the Thirteenth Judicial District courtroom of Judge Walter R. Heinrich in Tampa for her first appearance. To the consternation of Abraham's friends and family, Judge Heinrich granted Dee Dee's request for bond, but he set it at $1 million, with the caveat that Dee Dee would have to prove that any money she put up for bond had come into her possession legitimately.

Two days before Elizabeth Walker laid her son to rest, she sat with her spiritual advisor, the Reverend H. B. Holmes, and told reporters about the deceptive journey she had been led on by Dee Dee Moore. For months after Abraham's murder, Dee Dee and Elizabeth had travelled all over central Florida together, shopping, dining, and taking in various sights. Dee Dee had taken her to Busch Gardens. To Disney World. To the Holy Land Experience. To a New Year's Eve candlelight service in Plant City. Now, the bereaved mother said, she realized that Dee Dee's friendship had all been part of an act. "I can't understand how someone could do that knowing what has happened," she said. "Knowing that my son is dead and I'll never see him again."

But Reverend Holmes told the news conference he knew how Dee Dee had pulled it off. "She was the devil in disguise," he said.

On February 19, 2010, the Shakespeare family's worries that Dee Dee Moore would somehow make her extraordinary bond and slip confinement became moot when the state's attorney elevated the charge against her to murder in the first degree. Dee Dee was ordered held in Tampa's Orient Road Jail without bond. In March, a Hillsborough County grand jury returned a one-count indictment against Dee Dee Moore, charging her with murder "with a premeditated design to effect the death of Abraham Shakespeare or any other human being by shooting him, and during the commission of the offense, the said Dorice Donegan Moore carried, displayed, used, threatened to use, or attempted to use a weapon, to wit: a firearm, and actually possessed and discharged a firearm, and as a result of the discharge, death was inflicted upon Abraham Shakespeare." First-degree murder with premeditation gave the state's attorney the leeway to ask for the death penalty.

Lakeland's New Bethel A.M.E. Church sits majestically along Martin Luther King Jr. Avenue, a blond-and-white stucco edifice adorned with Celtic crosses and three arched front entrances to welcome the scores of mourners who would come the afternoon of Saturday, February 6, 2010, to bid Abraham Shakespeare farewell.

As Elizabeth Walker and her family entered the church, a choir sang several verses of "Soon and Very Soon," a black gospel favorite by Grammy Award–winning composer and recording artist Andraé Crouch. A long line of Abraham's friends trailed behind, among them Greg Smith, who was there to bid his old buddy farewell. He couldn't help but notice some of the curious stares he got from people who'd heard that he had somehow been involved with Dee Dee Moore's arrest but were not sure exactly what his role had been. Greg ignored the unsettling looks. He had come to pay his last respects.

The floral spray on the closed dark-cherrywood casket in front of the pulpit was a burst of white roses, orchids, chrysanthemums, and ferns. Perched on an easel nearby was a large photograph of Abraham in a suit and tie, looking reflective. Another photo on display featured a head-on shot of Abraham, his signature dreadlocks draping each shoulder.

Major Joe Halman, whom Cedric Edom had first contacted when he reported Abraham missing back in November, brought the congregation to its feet with applause when he introduced Dave Wallace and David Clark as the relentless detectives who'd broken the case. "They worked night and day around the clock as if this was their own family," Halman said of his men.

In his eulogy, Reverend Holmes portrayed Abraham as a Good Samaritan, whose kindness and generosity had cost him more than his millions.

"Sometimes doing good to others, you might find

yourself falling in the midst of bad people," said Reverend Holmes. "That's why you've got to have a connection with God so you don't have a connection with the wrong people. When we live a life of salvation we won't be tricked by the enemy."

A praise dancer in mime face moved fluidly to a recording of gospel mogul Kirk Franklin's rhythmic anthem, "The Storm Is Over Now."

> No more cloudy days
> They're all gone away
> I feel like I can make it
> The storm is over now.

As the service neared its end, Moses Shakespeare, the elder of Abraham's two sons, at eight years old, walked with his mother and an aunt to the front of the church.

"I want to thank everyone for coming to my dad's funeral," he said, his voice low and trembling. He was a good father, Moses said. "I just miss all the good times."

Immediately after the funeral, Abraham Lee Shakespeare was buried in the Oak Hill Burial Park, two hundred manicured acres managed by the city of Lakeland since 1926. Interred that day was a man who, for a brief while, was a multimillionaire but who died once more homeless and virtually penniless. His funeral cost the family less than $6,000. A few months later, a simple, placard-style headstone was laid to mark his final resting place. Along with his name and birth date it reads, "Safe in the arms of Jesus," and although the date of his death was never firmly established (even the grand-jury indictment only said "on or between April 1st and April 13th, 2009"), it lists April 7, 2009, as the day his life ended.

CHAPTER EIGHTEEN

·····

Far be it from Dee Dee Moore to sit back and lick her wounds just because she was behind bars, charged with first-degree murder. Held for trial at the Orient Road Jail, in Tampa, she continued to nurse fantasies of holding on to her house, jewelry, and other goods and, as usual, looked for accomplices. A few of her fellow inmates had promised that, once they were released, they would help Dee Dee carry out her plan to transfer ownership of her property and belongings to their names in another desperate quest to protect the goods from being seized by the courts. But none of the women followed through.

In late June 2010, Hillsborough County detective Preston Hollis went to the jail to see a short, stocky, thirty-year-old black woman named Angelina Marshall who was being held at Orient Road on a grand-theft charge. Jail authorities had told investigators that Angelina had information they might find useful in the continuing Dee Dee Moore case.

Angelina told Hollis she shared a section of the jail with Dee Dee and got to know her from conversations in the recreation yard. She was impressed by Dee Dee's "sincerity," even though other pod mates (like a woman everyone called Muffin) found Dee Dee's conflicting stories troubling. Angelina chalked that up to Dee Dee's fretfulness. After all, the "lottery killer"—Angelina's term—kept insisting that she was innocent and was actually taking the rap for someone else.

"I said, 'If you didn't do this, then why in the hell are you sitting in here?'" Angelina told Hollis. "Tell 'em who did it. She say, 'I can't.' I said, 'What you mean you can't? If somebody did something and I didn't do it, I'm not gonna sit in here and take the rap.'"

Hollis listened intently as Angelina recalled her conversations with her infamous fellow inmate. Follow-up questions were not necessary with this woman. She was on a roll from the start.

"She said, what happened was, her and R. J., which is her son, went and Abraham called her because he wanted to go do a drug transaction. He need the money outta the safe," said Angelina. Hollis knew that Dee Dee kept a safe in the office at 5732 State Road 60, the house where the shooting had occurred.

"She said they were arguing because she was trying to tell him, you know, 'You're going to do this and you know you're not gonna get your money back.' So, they was arguing back and forth," Angelina continued.

"Uh-huh," said Hollis.

"And she said that in the process, it got, the argument got out of control. She [said] 'R. J. is the one that took the gun out of the safe.' I said, 'How did he get the gun out of the safe; did he reach down and get the gun?' She say, 'No, the gun was on the side pocket when you open the door.'"

"Uh-huh."

"And she said that he always tote a gun with him—Abraham."

"Okay."

"And they was arguing. And she say he took the gun out of the back of his pants."

Hollis hadn't heard that one before. Abraham bringing a gun to the scene was a new twist. He listened intently as Angelina continued.

"And she say she don't know if he was gonna point it at her or he was gonna sit it down, but that's when R. J. grabbed the gun and shot him two times." Dee Dee told her that happened on April 6, 2009, Angelina said.

Hollis remained calm, even at this disturbing revelation that Dee Dee was resurrecting the claim that her teenage son had killed Abraham Shakespeare, an allegation detectives had debunked. He didn't want to react in any way that might cause Angelina to clam up. He wanted to hear what she had been told, no matter how outlandish.

"So I say, 'Well who buried him?'" Angelina went on. "She say that she called James . . .'"

"How did you know he was buried?" Hollis asked.

"Because she told me."

"Okay."

"She said she had called [her ex-husband] and explained to him what happened. He came over. And I said, 'Well what did you do with him, you just left him there?' She say, 'No, we put him in the garage in the closet to the next day,' which was the seventh. That's when they bury him, on the seventh."

"Okay."

"She say he came and he dug the hole—the husband, the ex-husband rather—he dug the hole. And I say, 'So he knew what had happened' and she said 'Yeah.' And then she started crying. I say, 'Well why you crying?' She say, 'Because it's not fair that now he's turning my son against me and now my son wants nothing to do with me. He won't write me. He won't talk to me on the phone. He's taking all of my stuff like I'm dead and sold it on eBay and Craigslist and the rest he just dropped off to my mom's house and told my mom to put it in a garage sale and it's just not fair.'"

Hollis knew it certainly sounded like something the self-pitying Dee Dee would say. Besides, Angelina could not have known some of the details unless Dee Dee, or someone very close to the case, had told her. The part about the garage closet was new, however.

"They had put his body in a closet in the garage?" Hollis asked, wanting more.

"In the garage. She say they drug him from the office to the garage and put it in a little closet that she had in the garage," Angelina said. "And then the next day, after he dug the hole, then the next day they went back and put him in the hole."

"Did she say that R. J. was there for that, too?" Hollis inquired.

"Yeah. She said she couldn't lift him by herself."

"Uh-huh."

"So I say, 'Well why didn't you just call and say, you know, we was arguing and it just got outta control?' She say she panicked and she just freaked out. And I said, 'Well, that make you accessory to that, you know?'"

"Uh-huh."

"And she say, 'I understand but I already know. I'm not telling on my son so I already know the most they can give me is fifteen to twenty-five.'" Apparently, Dee Dee was either badly misinformed or fooling herself. Fifteen- to twenty-five-year sentences fall within the state's norms for manslaughter, but Dee Dee was charged with first-degree murder, which carries a minimum sentence of twenty-five years in Florida.

Uninterrupted by the detective, Angelina continued spilling the beans.

"She say it was a million dollars in the safe," she said. "And I said, 'Well where is the money?' She say, 'I have the money buried.' So I say, 'You have the money buried?' She say, 'Yeah.' I said, 'Well what do you want from me?'"

"Uh-huh."

Angelina told Hollis that Dee Dee verbally gave her a long list of things to do and promised to write it all out for her when Angelina was about to be released from Orient Road. In the interim, Angelina said, Dee Dee had given her power of attorney and a jail sergeant had notarized it.

"It was power to turn over everything—her bank accounts, her businesses, her property, everything," Angelina said. "She said, 'I want you to go get the money out the bank.' She said, 'I want you to pay your seven thousand dollars off your restitution.' She say, 'I want you to make sure my mama gets three hundred dollars a week' 'cause that's what she was paying her mama when she was home. She say, ''cause my mama don't need to be struggling.'"

Hollis scribbled on his notepad as this new information poured from Angelina's mouth.

"And I say, 'Well what about the money that was in the safe?' She say, 'Once you get out and do what I tell you to do on the list of stuff that I'm gonna give you and I can trust you, then I tell you where the money at.' And I said, 'Well what do I suppose to do with the money?' She say R. J. turned sixteen in January. 'I want you to buy him a 2010 Ford Mustang. And make sure he have money until I come home. Once I come home, then you can transfer everything back over to me.'"

"Uh-huh."

"She want me to do a will so that if anything happened to me, I have to put in the will that she gets that stuff back, so my family won't try to take it."

"Did she mention what bank account, for what bank all the money's supposed to be in?" Hollis asked.

"She got several bank accounts."

"Oh."

Angelina told the detective that Dee Dee had also

instructed her to remove the paintball field equipment from behind the State Road properties. Dee Dee harped on it for so long that, eventually, Angelina lied and said her boyfriend had cleared the paintball field—a falsehood but one that had served its purpose in getting Dee Dee to silence at least that demand.

"So she was like, 'It worth sixty thousand dollars,'" Angelina rattled on. "'Once he sell it, he keeps half of the money and I want you to put me some money in my account.' And then she got her little list of stuff that she wants me to pay off, stuff she want me to order for her, stuff she want me to get for her mom and her son and stuff like that."

Hollis leaned back in his chair and took a deep breath. There were a few things he wanted to circle back on, beginning with the alleged argument with Abraham Shakespeare in the State Road office.

"Did she mention what the argument was about that they were arguing?" he asked.

"Because he was going to do a deal with somebody and she say she know he wasn't gonna get his money back," Angelina replied.

"Uh-huh."

"And she was like, one thing led to another and so she was, like, she opened up the safe and then they steady with exchanging words and it just got out of control. And I say, 'So what happened?' And she said that's when R. J. pulled the gun and shot."

Hollis flipped through his pad to return to his notes about the confrontation that fateful day.

"And I was like, 'Well why didn't you just call the police?' It would just been so simple, just call the police and say, 'Hey, look, we were arguing; he had a gun in his pocket, he took it out, my son got scared and my son just reacted.' Instead of just not saying anything for that long, you know?"

"Uh-huh. Uh-huh."

"And I'm like, 'How could you go to this place every single day knowing somebody buried in your backyard?' I said, 'It didn't smell?' And she was like, 'No, because we poured lime in there.' And I was like, 'Okay, lime is for fleas because I put that in my yard for my dogs when they get fleas, you know.' But she just looked blank."

"Hmmm."

"I was telling my sister, I'm like, 'I don't know what to do.' I say, 'I think this girl for real this time when she told me this because she looked it, so sincere and she was just so . . . I think she was more hurt this time because the son just like don't want nothing to do with her no more. He's not talking to her, he don't write, he don't call, he done got what he wanted and put it on eBay or whatever and sold it. The rest he drops off at the grandma house and then the daddy girlfriend's wearing all her stuff.' So I think that's what really hurt her the most."

Hollis couldn't help but shake his head over the idea that Dee Dee would blame her young son for something else. Selling her things online without her permission? The detective decided then and there that it wasn't even worth looking into. Dee Dee had already tried to pin

Abraham's murder on her only child. He didn't find it surprising or even intriguing that she would accuse him of profiting off his mother's misfortunes.

Hollis glanced at his notes and then at Angelina. She had a lot of information—stuff only an intimate of the case would know. The discovery of Abraham's remains and Dee Dee's subsequent arrest had certainly garnered a lot of media attention, but Angelina Marshall did not impress him as someone who followed news accounts diligently. Plus, some of the details she imparted had not yet been publicly disclosed. Moreover, some of what Angelina was telling him was not known by even the detectives, like the buried money and "several" bank accounts.

And, now, according to Angelina, there was one more potential treasure trove.

"She got a storage," she said. "She want me to go to her storage and get everything out the storage and let her mama go through it all."

If any of these secret stashes existed, Hollis knew his visit to the Orient Road Jail had been well worthwhile, giving law enforcement another lead or two. If they were figments of Dee Dee's overwrought imagination, the stories would at least give investigators more insight into how the crooked wheels were turning in Dee Dee's head.

"I told her that they had seized some of her stuff 'cause I see it on the news and was talking about it," Angelina reported. "And she was like, 'Oh no. I got stuff they don't even know about.' And I was like, 'Oh okay.'"

With his time winding down, Hollis had a few last questions for the talkative informant.

"You know of anybody else that she's close with?" he asked.

"I'm the only one she's freaking close with," Angelina said emphatically.

"Okay. Do y'all have roommates?"

Angelina revealed that Dee Dee had talked about the case with her in the presence of a roommate but said she had reassured Dee Dee that the roommate was "cool; she ain't gonna say nothing."

"Uh-huh," said Hollis, waiting for more.

"And she was like, 'Okay.' And then she started talking in front of her. But, see, this girl is not even from here."

"Who's your roommate? What's her name?"

"Uh, Pauley. Deanna Pauley. Yeah, but she done talked in front of Deanna and she done talked in front of Muffin, too, 'cause me and Muffin real close. And I tell her . . . They ain't gonna say nothing, these my friends. And she'll sit down and then she'll start telling."

CHAPTER NINETEEN

·····

The trial of *State of Florida versus Dorice Donegan Moore* began in Tampa at 9:00 A.M. on November 26, 2012, just over six years after Abraham Shakespeare won the lottery, three and a half years after he was killed, and almost three years after his decomposing remains were dug up from Dee Dee Moore's backyard. The courtroom was filled with prospective jurors, reporters, Abraham's relatives and friends, and curious townspeople who had come to witness the culmination of a case that had captured the public fascination for years.

Judge Emmett Lamar Battles, a retired U.S. Army colonel with ten years on the Thirteenth Judicial Circuit Court bench, presided. Wiry and intense, James Jay Pruner, chief of the Major Crimes Division in the state's attorney's office and a recognized expert in homicide cases, readied the prosecution. Two men flanked the defendant Dee Dee

Moore: Christopher Boldt and Byron Hileman, both accustomed to high-profile cases. They had taken the case after the public defender's office withdrew, citing an unspecified "ethical conflict." A 2007 Florida law had established "regional counsel" offices in each of the state's five appellate districts to represent indigent defendants when the public defender's office cannot or will not, as in Dee Dee's case.

The public had not heard from Dee Dee Moore in two years—not since the *Tampa Tribune* reported on her jailhouse phone call to the newspaper in September 2010, protesting her innocence and insisting that she feared for her and her son's life, and a Tampa television station reported in December 2010 that it had received a stack of handwritten jailhouse letters from her, along with excerpts from a book she said she was writing, titled *One Step Closer to Crazy.*

In the letters, Dee Dee maintained that she had never harmed Abraham Shakespeare, only helped him, and that she had believed the hole in her backyard—dug by the mysterious Ronald and another man—was intended for burying what was left of Abraham's money. Once again, she claimed that threats to her son's life had been what led her to mislead investigators. She also complained about memory loss, chest pains, and poor treatment in jail.

Observers found that the Dee Dee Moore who came to trial at the end of November 2012 had lost weight during her incarceration at the Orient Road Jail while awaiting trial. They also noted that she was no longer bleaching her hair and instead now sported long, wavy dark tresses, some of which she had pinned up toward the crown of her head, away from her face. One prospective juror claimed not to recognize Dee Dee at first; so would a witness who had once worked for her.

More than a hundred men and women had been summoned for possible jury duty, all subject to voir dire, during which, predictably, both the prosecution and defense were most concerned with how much potential jurors knew about the case and whether they had already reached any presumptive conclusions.

The first person interviewed was Roger Gaines, a seventy-one-year-old retiree from Plant City.

"I saw it on the news when the gentleman was killed," Roger said. "And then I remember when [his body] was found in Plant City because I live in Plant City. So it caught my attention but that's the extent of it."

"As a result of publicity that you were exposed to at or near the time this all happened," Prosecutor Jay Pruner asked, "have you developed a fixed or definite opinion as to Miss Moore's either guilt or innocence in this matter?" No, Roger said, he had not.

"Do you know people that know Miss Moore?" asked defense attorney Byron Hileman when it was his turn to question the prospective juror.

"No."

"Did you talk with anyone in Plant City about what had happened once the body was discovered, just gossiping?"

"No, not at all."

"If you were chosen for the jury during the course of the trial you may remember things that you don't remember right now, like something is brought up and you reckon, 'Oh, yeah; I heard about that.' If that were to happen to you, do you think that you would be able to set that aside, whatever you read or heard, and make your decision based only on the evidence this judge tells you that you can consider here in the courtroom?"

"I can do it, and my knowledge of it is very limited. It's more like the headline on the news. So it's very limited, but to answer the question: yes, I could."

By day two, the prosecution and defense had interviewed about a third of the panel of prospects and had agreed on eight men, four women, and two female alternates to hear the case, with Roger Gaines of Plant City, the first interviewed, elected foreman. The panel was told to prepare for a two-week trial.

The prosecutor began his opening statement with the timeline of Abraham's association with Dee Dee Moore. There would be a lot of twists and turns in the story, and Pruner wanted to give the jurors an overall feel for how the tragic tale unfolded.

"Soon after Dee Dee Moore met Abraham Shakespeare, she became his financial advisor," Pruner said. "And within ninety days of that meeting, she had taken control of every asset that Abraham Shakespeare had left, his last million five, the house on Redhawk Bend, and the debts that he had out on the street. It didn't take long for Dee Dee Moore to taste the financial largess of Mr. Shakespeare. On January 2nd of 2009, a matter of weeks after she met Mr. Shakespeare, there was an electronic transfer of $246,000 from Abraham Shakespeare's Bank of America account into an account at Bank of America held in the name of a company called

American Medical Professionals, sometimes referred to by its acronym, AMP.

"American Medical Professionals, the evidence will show you, was a medical nursing staffing company that Miss Moore had for a few years. And in fact, Miss Moore had made a living at that company. The evidence will show you, according to what Miss Moore told investigators, by January 15th of 2009, Abraham Shakespeare was fearful that he could lose whatever he had remaining to Torrie Butler, the mother of his child, in child support litigation. The evidence will show you that this defendant fanned the flames of that fear.

"And so on January 15th of 2009, there is a document called an Assets Purchase Agreement signed by Miss Moore and Abraham Shakespeare. What that document purports to do is transfer to Miss Moore the right to collect all of the outstanding loans that Mr. Shakespeare had on the street in exchange for $185,000 from Miss Moore to Mr. Shakespeare. And as the evidence will show you, it was a transaction that amounted to payment of value of eight cents on the dollar. On that same date, Mr. Shakespeare purportedly sold the home at Redhawk Bend in Lakeland to Miss Moore for $685,000. The total transaction or money owed by Miss Moore to Mr. Shakespeare was $870,000 for those two transactions."

By early February 2009, Pruner said, all that remained of Abraham's fortune was a $1,095,000 annuity with Prudential Life Insurance Company. Dee Dee wasted no time setting up Abraham Shakespeare, Limited Liability Corporation, with Abraham, Judith Haggins, and

Dorice Moore as its officers. She opened a bank account for the LLC the next day and promptly transferred the Prudential proceeds into the new account.

"But what you will hear from Doug Hancock, the branch manager who opened the account, is that after Mr. Shakespeare had walked out the door of the bank, Ms. Moore came back in and said, 'Don't give him'—meaning Mr. Shakespeare—'any access to that money.'"

As soon as the annuity funds were available, Pruner said, Dee Dee began making substantial withdrawals. Furthermore, the prosecutor said, "the evidence will show you that within sixty days of having been divested of everything that he owns to Dee Dee Moore, all that's left of Abraham Shakespeare is his decaying body in a grave under a concrete slab behind a house that she bought on Highway 60 near Plant City, Florida."

Having set the scene of Dee Dee's alleged fraud and deceit, the assistant state's attorney would next take the jurors through the labyrinth of rumors, excuses, and alibis that Dee Dee and others had constructed to delay and frustrate the search for Abraham Shakespeare.

The courtroom was pin-drop quiet as Pruner exposed the web of deceit that had ensnared Abraham Shakespeare's fate and fortune. As the prosecutor spoke, Dee Dee scribbled furiously, shoving notes in front of her attorneys.

Pruner went on. "The evidence will show you, ladies and gentlemen, that this defendant killed Abraham Shakespeare; that she had the body, the motive to do so; that she killed him with her own gun," he said, coming to the end of a long and winding opening statement. "She admits in interviews with law enforcement that it was her gun that was used to kill Abraham Shakespeare, but indicates it wasn't her, it was one of many other people she named. She buried him on her property and she took extreme, calculated steps to avoid detection, apprehension, and the truth."

Defense attorney Byron Hileman, rising on Dee Dee's behalf, was considerably briefer. He conceded that the "evidence and documents are what they are" but said that the state's murder case against his client was circumstantial.

"For example," said Hileman, "you will find that all of the evidence that is presented here, there are no eyewitnesses who can testify that Miss Moore shot and killed Mr. Shakespeare, or was present when he was shot and killed, or had any part in carrying out his murder." Even the abundance of incriminating audiotapes and videotapes were dubious, Hileman said, and he urged the jurors to question the many recordings they were going to hear.

"She at no point either admits or implies that she killed Mr. Shakespeare or had any part in helping anyone else to do so," Hileman told the panel. "She also imparts to them that what she does know about what might have happened, which is only partial knowledge, she has not freely shared with them because her life and the life of her son had been threatened by the people responsible and she's frightened. And that is stated to the police repeatedly. We believe if you listen to all of that evidence, it will become clear that she set forth her version of what she knows. Police did not accept it, and they're asking you to draw inferences from the facts here that are one possible explanation, but only one."

With that, the stage was set for a trial that would ultimately produce thirty witnesses and dozens of exhibits. The prosecution would try to prove that Dee Dee took control of Abraham's assets, killed and buried him, and schemed to throw skeptics and investigators off her trail. The defense, meanwhile, would portray Dee Dee Moore as a perhaps clumsy but well-meaning financial advisor and friend to Abraham and someone who'd been left to clean up a mess when he disappeared. Lacking hard evidence, the defense put forth that any suggestion Dee Dee had done harm to Abraham was sheer conjecture.

The state opened its case with James Moore, Dee Dee's former husband of sixteen years and father of her only child, R. J. The couple had divorced in 2009.

The stocky, brown-haired man stepped to the witness stand and explained that a couple of years earlier, he had used his excavation equipment to clear a swath of land on Dee Dee's State Road 60 properties in preparation for the construction of a paintball field, his ex-wife's new business venture. Then in early April 2009, he picked up a used backhoe that Dee Dee had purchased at an auction and delivered it to her.

"During sometime in April of 2009, did you use the backhoe that you had transported to the defendant's properties on Highway 60 to dig a hole?" Pruner asked.

"Yes," James replied.

"Okay. Tell us how that came about."

"She called me one afternoon, told me that she had

some debris and stuff from the house that she was remodeling and needed to bury it and asked me to come dig the hole. So I went over and I dug it."

"What did you use to dig it?"

"The backhoe that she owned."

"Do you recall what time of day it would have been?"

"It was late in the afternoon."

Pruner presented a series of photographs of the State Road properties, focusing on a white door on the back of the house at 5732.

"About how close in terms of distance did Miss Moore want you to dig this hole near this door on the back of the redbrick house, approximately?" Pruner inquired.

"Five feet probably," James said.

"What did you tell her about what you thought about that idea?"

"I was worried that there could be electrical or water lines and that I wouldn't dig it there."

"What happened after you told her that?"

"She walked over here to the other piece of property and showed me other spots where we should dig the hole." Aided by more photographs, James pointed out a plot of land near a stand of trees behind the split-level house at 5802. With Dee Dee beside him, James said, he used the backhoe to dig a hole to her liking, then left and went home. Two or three hours later, Dee Dee asked him to come back and fill in the hole.

"She looked like she had been working," James said of his return. "She was real sweaty, like she had been working."

"Okay," said Pruner. "And what did you do when you returned?"

"I got on the backhoe and I pushed the dirt back in the hole."

"Did you pay attention to what was in the hole?"

"No."

"Did you see any debris in there?"

"As far as I remember there was, but I'm not positive."

"Do you recall seeing a body in there?"

"No sir."

"Did you see anyone other than the defendant on that property when you returned to fill in the property later the same night that you dug the hole?"

"No sir."

On cross-examination, Hileman concentrated on James Moore's inability to say just what was in the hole he had dug at Dee Dee's request.

"You could see in the hole, couldn't you?" Hileman asked.

"Somewhat," said James. "With the canopy of the trees and it being dark, it was hard to see. I didn't walk up and inspect it. I just got on the machine and pushed the dirt."

"So it was dark but not pitch-black?"

"Right."

"Okay. Other than [Dee Dee's] appearance that you described as being looking as if she had been working, physically working, was there any other thing that you noted about her behavior or appearance that was unusual to you?"

"No sir."

Later that day, Pruner called a cement contractor to the stand, the man who had poured the driveway at 5802 State Road 60 on April 3, 2009. He recalled that, several days later, Dee Dee asked him to return to the property because she wanted him to pour a thirty-by-thirty-foot concrete slab in the backyard. Defense counsel Christopher Boldt homed in on the contractor's uncertainty about the exact date on which he'd poured the slab in Dee Dee's backyard.

"When was that requested?" Boldt asked. "That's what I'm not clear."

"I think it was a Thursday or Friday that she called me back and she wanted the job to get done. And I said, 'Okay, I'll get it done Monday,' you know, I'll send my guys and I'll schedule the concrete and we pour it that day."

"Did she show you where to put, where she wanted the thirty-by-thirty slab, the second job, when you were doing the first job?"

She had not, the contractor said.

The second day of testimony in the trial introduced the first of several lengthy audio recordings of police interviews with Dee Dee Moore, beginning with Christopher Lynn, the Polk County Sheriff's Office homicide detective who first interviewed Dee Dee three days after the missing person's report was filed and who had been tasked with investigating the maze of financial dealings between Dee Dee's companies and Abraham Shakespeare, LLC. Jurors heard Dee Dee tell Lynn that she had no documentation for the supposed sale of the house on Redhawk Bend Drive and that rather than pay Abraham outright for the house, she bought him airline and cruise tickets to pay off the $685,000.

The afternoon brought Abraham's mother, Elizabeth Walker, to the stand. In a soft and weary voice, she told the court about her son's last visit.

"I had told him that my CD player had broke," she said. "He said, 'Mom, you can have mine.' And he brought it over that afternoon. And he set it up and he didn't stay long. And when he walked out the door, I haven't seen him since."

Days, then weeks went by without a word from Abraham, Elizabeth said. "I was calling him and calling him and calling him, and he never did answer his phone. It started going to the voice mail and all and then I began to feel like he . . . maybe he was too busy; he didn't want to be bothered. So I just stopped calling." At one point, she said, Dee Dee—who by then had become something of a fixture in her life—told her that Abraham was sick and hospitalized.

"Is there any time that you were in Dee Dee Moore's Hummer where the two of you were talking about Abraham Shakespeare?" Pruner asked.

"Yes," Elizabeth said.

"What do you recall about that conversation?"

"One time we were talking and she stopped talking and got real silent. And all of a sudden, she said, 'And when he died.' So I looked over and I said, 'Well, what you mean when he died?' And she said, 'Oh, nothing.' She started talking. So I begin to feel suspicious about something. And I said within myself, 'Maybe he do have AIDS, and he's somewhere in a hospital or somewhere sick, you know, and maybe he done died and she just hadn't told me about it.'"

The packed courtroom hushed when Gregory Todd Smith, the state's star witness, strode to the witness stand on the afternoon of November 30, 2012, impeccable in a dress shirt and tie, dress slacks, and dress shoes, his hair and goatee freshly trimmed. It was a big difference from the casual "street" way he'd dressed—mainly in jeans and T-shirts—during the months of escapades with Dee Dee.

Soon after Dee Dee's arrest, Greg had returned to his barber business in Lakeland and to the customers he had not been able to regularly service during the time he'd been embroiled in efforts to nab Dee Dee. Likewise, he'd kick-started his handyman business, a sideline that kept him on the move for home owners in need of repair or restoration work. Despite these preoccupations and his now well-reported role in the investigation of Dee Dee Moore, Greg was well aware that not everyone had a positive impression of his involvement in the case. He'd heard the speculation about whether he had been in cahoots with Dee Dee, about whether he had been intimately involved with her, about whether he had benefitted from Abraham's death. On a few occasions, when a question about his role seemed genuine, he had taken on the skeptic to dispel his or her doubts. But anyone who appeared to be spreading innuendo—moreover, enjoying the discomfort it wrought—got a good telling-off from the streetwise man, who'd never been known to tolerate being messed with. Even during the trial, with its treasury of damning evidence against Dee Dee, rumors persisted that Greg had had a hand in Abraham's sad fate—a suspicion the defense tried but failed to exploit and that the state's attorney, the investigating officers, and the prevailing evidence had ruled out as pure fiction.

Before his time came on the stand, Greg had pulled Elizabeth Walker aside in the witness holding room.

"How do you think it's going?" he asked Abraham's mother.

She told him she was worried that Dee Dee Moore would be acquitted.

"Well, do you know who I am?" Greg inquired. Elizabeth looked at him quizzically. "I'm the guy who got Dee Dee Moore to give up the information," he said. "I don't want you to worry about this. We're going to get her." Then he apologized to the dead man's mother for some of the ways he talked about her son in his role as Dee Dee's confidante, as captured on audio recordings and transcripts.

"Those tapes have me saying some pretty awful things," he explained. "I just want to tell you that I'm sorry, and that I didn't mean none of those things. I just had to pretend some things in order to get Dee Dee to feel comfortable with me so she would talk."

Elizabeth told Greg that she understood, and she thanked him for the work he had done.

If he was nervous as he entered the crowded courtroom, Greg didn't show it. Nor did he acknowledge the defendant. Throughout the three days he would spend on the stand, Greg studiously avoided even looking in the direction of the woman he had befriended under false pretenses, the woman who had led him to Abraham's body.

For hours, jurors listened to Greg's recordings of his meetings with Dee Dee. They heard the planning to purchase cell phones, registering the accounts under fake names in hopes of throwing detectives off the trail; the hours in the Comfort Inn creating a bogus letter to Abraham's mother; the ride to Elizabeth Walker's neighborhood to deliver the letter; Dee Dee's incessant talk about the people Abraham wanted to avoid, especially "Ronald" and Cedric; and the fictitious young prostitute pressing charges against him for assault. They heard Dee Dee's grousing about police suspicions and interrogations. They heard the duo's conversation about finding someone to take the fall for killing Abraham. And they heard the plan to retrieve Abraham's body from beneath the concrete slab.

"Did you ever go back to that property to attempt to remove the body of Abraham Shakespeare?" the prosecutor asked Greg.

"No."

"Did you see the defendant later that night?"

"Yes."

"All right. Under what circumstances?"

"We was getting ready to get arrested together so they can take her in custody. And they was trying to figure out how to get her out of the house or whatever. So I told them I would make a phone call and tell them . . . tell her that there's a whole lot of polices down there, 'What did you do, set me up? I need to talk to you.' So I did that. She came out of the house. She met me at the mall, Lakeland Mall in front of Dillard's, and the police came and got both of us."

"Did they allow her to drive her own car down to the police station?"

"Yes."

"Did you drive your own car down to the police station?"

"Yes."

"Did you have any conversation with the defendant during that drive?"

"Yes."

"How was that done?"

"Telephone."

"Who called who?"

"She called me."

"Do you recall what she said in that conversation?"

"She just told me not to say anything, keep my mouth closed and don't worry about it."

"Did she say to blame it on anybody if it were to get to that point?"

"Yeah, said we got to blame it on the guy Ronald."

"Was there a point in the conversation when you talked to Dee Dee and explained that you were going to bury the remains of Mr. Shakespeare after burning his remains with kerosene?"

"Yes."

"At that point did Miss Moore tell you that you better give him some marshmallows?"

"Yeah," Greg said, feeling the same knot in his stomach that he had felt when Dee Dee made the reprehensible joke back in 2010.

The treasury of lengthy, candid recordings and the fact that Greg had been working with the police all along made him a powerful witness, notwithstanding his own criminal record. He had extracted details from Dee Dee that no one else had been able to get. The defense would have to discredit him if there was any hope of the jury discounting the tapes. Hileman stepped up.

"Why would you spend that much time, that much energy, your gas money, travel time, doing all of the things you did?" the defense counsel asked sternly. "What did you stand to gain from that?"

"That was my friend," Greg said. "I was trying to find out where he at and what's wrong."

"You're not trying to frame Miss Moore?"

"Man, I didn't care about framing Miss Moore."

"That is what you're doing, though isn't it?"

A sustained objection cut the tension. Hileman regrouped only to be stopped by the judge again when the tone of his questions suggested that Greg's history with drug dealing might have been a factor in his involvement with Dee Dee. Hileman took another tact.

"You aren't the one that volunteered that 'I've got a friend that I know being in a lot of trouble?'" he asked, zooming in on the fall-guy episode.

"I sure did, because she asked me for it," Greg said.

"It was your idea, wasn't it?"

"No, it wasn't my idea."

Then Hileman moved in for the kill.

"Were you involved in any way in the disappearance of Mr. Shakespeare?"

"No, I wasn't," Greg said firmly.

"Did you have any knowledge of people who were involved?"

"No, I didn't." Uncowed by the attorney's barrage, Greg kept his answers simple and clipped.

"Just to recap," Hileman continued, "you spent a lot of time between December 28th and January 26th, I believe, working with and for the police in this case, isn't that correct?"

"Yes."

"Because you were anxious to find your friend Shakespeare?"

"Exactly."

"But between the time that he is alleged to have disappeared in April until December, you didn't do anything to try to find your friend Mr. Shakespeare, did you?"

"I didn't know where he was. All I know is he could have went anywhere. He had money. The word on the streets, somebody put on the streets, he was on a cruise. He was in Orlando. He was in Miami. . . . He was in Texas. There was a whole lot of hearsay about where he was."

"Can I get a direct answer?" Hileman shot back. "You didn't do anything, did you?"

Despite the prosecutor's objections, Judge Battles directed Greg to answer the question. It was hard to miss the disgust in Greg's voice as he was forced to answer the annoying question.

"No, I didn't do anything," he said.

On redirect, the prosecutor steered the jury's attention back to the circumstances that had put Greg Smith in Dee Dee Moore's orbit in the first place and away from Hileman's insinuations that the informant stood to benefit from Abraham's absence, given that he owed the man money.

"The attorney that wrote you the letter claiming that you were in arrears on the debt, was that Howard Stitzel?" Pruner asked.

"Yes," Greg said.

"Did they ever take you to court?"

"No."

"Did Mr. Stitzel or Miss Moore ever foreclose on the property?"

"No."

"After you contacted Miss Moore and spoke to her about it, was there any further action taken to attempt to enforce any default?"

"No."

"During this time that you were cooperating with police, did you still own your barbershop?"

"Yes."

"Did you still have it open?"

"Yes."

"Were you still cutting hair and working when you weren't with Miss Moore and the police?"

"It's not only that; I got seven people that work for me."

His testimony and work on the case finally done, Greg stepped off the stand and walked out of the courtroom, passing Dee Dee Moore without so much as a glance her way.

CHAPTER TWENTY

·····

Shar Krasniqi moved quietly and steadily toward the witness stand. He was now twenty-nine years old, living in Atlanta and a newlywed, having married a nurse named Paige earlier that year, in May 2012. His testimony came on the eighth day of trial.

Shar told the court that in addition to his role as boyfriend, he had assisted Dee Dee with her medical staffing business, mainly handling payroll, and had helped renovate the house at 5732 State Road 60 when Dee Dee opened her office there in the fall of 2008. He had also performed some handyman duties at the house next door, the 5802 address, when Dee Dee bought it in late April 2009 for $253,000, titling the deed in Shar's name.

"Did Miss Moore ever explain to you how she was able to afford to buy the residence at 5802 State Road 60?" state's attorney James Pruner asked.

"When I asked her, she explained that she received some money from a Whistleblower Act, something from the IRS." Shar said calmly.

"Did she give you an idea of how much money and how many settlements she had received from the IRS as a whistle-blower?"

"She said twice that she had done this and each time it was over $310,000."

"Prior to that conversation, did you have any idea what whistle-blowers or whistle-blowing did or what it was?"

"No, I did not."

"Did you accept and take that explanation at face value?"

"I did."

Shar recalled first meeting Abraham Shakespeare at the beginning of 2009, when Dee Dee sent Shar to Abraham's Redhawk Bend Drive home to repair a broken outdoor spigot.

"From your contacts with Mr. Shakespeare, did you draw any impressions about his mental abilities?" Pruner asked Dee Dee's former lover.

"He didn't strike me as very intelligent," Shar said. "You know, just through our few conversations, he didn't come across very smart."

Shar testified that he saw Abraham only two or three times after that first meeting, but, thereafter, the tall, lanky multimillionaire loomed large in Dee Dee's life.

"Did you notice any difference or change in Miss Moore's involvement in the day-to-day operations of

American Medical Professionals after you knew that she had met and developed some type of relationship with Mr. Shakespeare?"

"Yes, the more she would hang out with Abraham, the less she would spend time with her business."

"Did that translate into any change or in the amounts of money that you saw coming through payroll?"

"It changed the amount of people that I paid. So, subsequently, I guess it would have changed the amount of money coming in."

Calmly, the young man recalled how he'd proudly showed off a wooden swing he had stained and mounted in a tree behind the redbrick house on State Road 60 as a Valentine's Day gift to Dee Dee in February 2009. After thanking him, she drove Shar to a Chevrolet dealership, where she pointed out a new $70,000 Corvette, telling him, "That's your gift." He picked it up a week later, paid in full. Six weeks later, Dee Dee purchased a large Chevy truck from the same dealership and titled it in Shar's name, too.

"What did you do with that vehicle?" Pruner asked, referring to the swanky sports car.

"Once the detectives informed me that it was purchased with money probably taken from Mr. Shakespeare, I wanted to return it," he said. Detectives confirmed that Shar had turned the vehicle over to them.

The defense used Shar's testimony to portray Dee Dee as a generous and appreciative person. In addition to the Corvette, Dee Dee had treated Shar to a Rolex watch, Las Vegas vacations, a fancy title in her company, and all-expenses-paid cohabitation. She had also allowed Shar's mother, Patricia, and another former AMP employee to live in the house at 5732 State Road 60 for free when they were down on their luck.

In her subsequent testimony, Patricia would confirm that Dee Dee could be thoughtful and generous. But she also said that the woman could do peculiar things, as she did on January 25, 2010—the day that Dee Dee told Greg where Abraham's body was buried.

That afternoon, Patricia said, she had helped Dee Dee empty the trailer hitched to a white truck driven onto the property at 5802 State Road 60. Although she wondered why Dee Dee was in such a hurry to unload the truck, Patricia said she was more concerned with why Dee Dee wanted to turn off the elaborate lighting and security cameras that surrounded the property. Patricia was still living in the property next door at 5732 at the time.

"Why did you think that was odd?" prosecutor Pruner inquired.

"Because it was always on; 24/7 it was on. She wanted everything monitored. And I asked her about it and said, 'Why are you turning them off?' And she said she was trying to save electricity."

"Did Miss Moore want any other lighting turned off to which you objected?"

"She did. She asked that the inside lights in the house be shut off as well. This was prior to us leaving. It was starting to get dark and my cat was in the house, and I said, 'Absolutely not, I'm not leaving my cat in the dark.' It didn't make any sense to me."

Patricia said that in the evening of that same day, she and her housemate went to Dee Dee's house on Redhawk Bend Drive for some good food and conversation, a movie and a sleepover—a "girls' night," she called it. Shar was going to make spaghetti for them.

"Did you have dinner at the Redhawk home with your son and Dee Dee Moore?"

"No, I don't know if he ever got it cooked that night or not. That was the goal, the intention."

"Did Miss Moore stay at that residence on Redhawk Bend in Lakeland the entire evening of January 25th of 2010?"

"No, she was there about an hour and then she came and told us and said Judy broke down somewhere and she needed to go and leave and go help her."

"How long did you stay there?"

"It was just a few minutes after she left that I left. I went upstairs and talked to Shar and said, 'Something is wrong.'"

Patricia said that when she got back to her home on State Road 60, she found it surrounded by sheriffs' deputies, who would not let her in.

Aside from the six-inch-long bejeweled earrings that hung from her lobes, brushing her neck and shoulders, Judith Haggins looked plain and somber as she approached the witness stand.

Her friendship with Abraham Shakespeare went back fifteen years, she said, and after he won the lottery and gave away so much of his winnings, she helped him collect his debts, issued receipts, and drove him and his mother around. It was at Abraham's new house in Lakeland that she first met Dee Dee Moore, who told Judy that she was writing a book about Abraham's good fortune. Judy was impressed with the professionally dressed woman, who said she owned a medical staffing company that brought in about $850,000 a year. As far as Judy could tell, Dee Dee seemed qualified to assist her old friend in managing his newfound riches.

"Did you ever talk with Miss Moore about her having created or formed an entity called Abraham Shakespeare, LLC, limited liability corporation?" the state's attorney asked.

"As I recall, I don't recall talking to her about it, but it was mentioned."

"Did you know that you were a board member of an entity that was created by Miss Moore called Abraham Shakespeare, LLC?"

"Not as I know of."

Judy professed to having no knowledge of, part in, or understanding of the assorted funds that were transferred between Abraham's and Dee Dee's LLCs. Then Pruner showed her the power of attorney that bore her name.

"To your understanding, what did that document allow you to do?" Pruner asked.

"To my understanding, to receive—take charge—if anything, that if he wasn't here, that I can act on his behalf," said Judy.

"Including collecting debts?"

"Debts, also."

"Did you ever see Abraham Shakespeare after April third of 2009, when he signed that power of attorney?"

"Yes, I did."

"And when in relation to April third did you see Mr. Shakespeare the next time?"

"It had to be April the fifth."

"And where was that, ma'am?"

"At his home on Redhawk, where he lived on Redhawk."

She, Abraham, and Dee Dee were supposed to get together at the Hard Rock casino in Tampa the next night, but he never showed, Judy said. After several failed attempts to reach them, Judy finally got a call from Dee Dee around midnight.

"She told me about Abraham had got in trouble," she testified. "Something had happened to Abraham that night and he supposed to have been with a young lady. And she supposed to have taken some money from him, [he] supposed to have choked her, and the lady was supposed to have went to the hospital. And they wanted me to go to try to find out what she did. But [Dee Dee] couldn't tell me who was the lady, couldn't tell me the person's name. So, how could I go to the hospital and check?"

Without further ado, Pruner fast-forwarded the witness nine months to January 2010, eliciting an affirmative response when he asked Judy Haggins if she knew then that the Polk County Sheriff's Office was investigating Abraham's whereabouts. Pruner then asked Judy about a phone call she'd received from Dee Dee Moore in the early morning hours of January 26.

"She called me and she woke me up and she said, 'Hey, I need to tell you something.' And I said, 'Okay. What?'" Judy began. "She said, 'I really need to tell you Abraham is dead.' So I jumped up and I said, 'Hold on, hold on.' And she said, 'Yes?' and I said, 'Are you serious?' And she said, 'Yes.' And so I said, 'Well, how long has he been dead?' And she say, 'You remember you supposed to have met us at the casino and he didn't show that day?' And I said, 'You f'ing played me and his mother.' And I just lost it. But I had to remember that I need to come back so I can find out more. So I started talking to her and she started telling me that what happened . . . I asked her, 'So what happened?' and she stated that the drug dealer made her tell me this and text me backward and forward so that Abraham was actually dead. She said the drug dealer made her tell me, that he wanted [Abraham] to write a check for $200,000 and he said he wasn't going to do it. She said he had a gun to her head."

"Who had a gun to her head?" Pruner asked.

"Abraham. She said Abraham had a gun to her head and because she didn't want to write the check, she said she blanked out and when she came to, he was shot. And I kept saying, 'That's not true, Abraham don't do drugs. He wasn't in drugs.' She said, 'Yes, he was. He just didn't want you to know that.' I said, 'Dee Dee, that's not true.'"

When it was his turn to question Haggins, Defense Attorney Hileman picked up where the witness had left off in her earlier testimony about Dee Dee's version of the shooting.

"Was anyone present, according to her story, other than herself, Mr. Shakespeare, and these drug dealers that she described?" he asked.

"She said Ronald and Cedric."

Doug Hancock had been the manager of the Bank of America branch where Dee Dee and Abraham had showed up on February 10, 2010, to open a new business checking account for Abraham Shakespeare, LLC. Dee Dee told Hancock that she was trying to help Abraham ward off some potential legal problems with the IRS and that they would soon fund the account with a substantial deposit. Hancock said that Dee Dee returned the very next day with Abraham, Judy Haggins, and purported minutes from a meeting of the LLC principals, noting that Abraham's name would be added to the new Bank of America account.

"During that meeting, did Mr. Shakespeare express an interest to have access to the money that he deposited?" Pruner asked Hancock, who was a witness for the state.

"Yes, sir. He was very adamant to insist that he was going to be able to get his money," Hancock replied. Pruner then showed the jury State's Exhibit 63B, a copy of a check from Prudential Annuities Life Assurance Company in the amount of $1,095,108.98. Under the agreement with the bank, both Dee Dee and Abraham could access the funds without the other's involvement.

"Did Miss Moore indicate to you how she met Abraham Shakespeare and what she was intending to do?" Pruner asked.

"She told me initially that what she did would basically head-hunt people that maybe were delinquent in IRS monies . . . and she would find them and basically turn them in to the IRS for the whistle-blower finder's fee," Hancock said. "And then she told me that once she got to know [Abraham], she was going to be writing a book about his life. And she started to feel sorry for him, so she was going to help him straighten everything out with the IRS."

Hancock told the court that once their business was done, Dee Dee and Abraham headed toward the door, then Dee Dee doubled back.

"She came back in to talk to me and say basically what she was wanting to communicate is that she did not want him to have access to the money and to please call her first before I ever let him get to any of the money," Hancock testified. "She was telling me that because he owed so much that he didn't know how much he really owed, that he was really broke. So that if he got access to the money, he would waste it and she wouldn't be able to help him. So she really didn't trust him to access the money."

Hancock explained that on February 12, 2009—two days after she had opened the account and one day after the Prudential check was deposited—Dee Dee asked him to remove Abraham Shakespeare's name altogether as a signatory on the new account. Five days later, she handed the bank manager what she said were minutes from another meeting of the LLC principals, this one authorizing the bank to delete Abraham's name as a signatory. The minutes listed Dee Dee as the sole attendee at the meeting.

"Does that document list the purported reason that Abraham Shakespeare, LLC, decided to remove Abraham Shakespeare as an authorized signatory on that account?" asked Pruner.

"Yes, sir," said Hancock. "It says, 'Decision was based on the discovery of criminal activity and attempt to defraud. Investigation is still going on and charges may follow. Refused involvement once I was made aware of his criminal intent.'" With that, Hancock said, he had Abraham's name removed as a signatory on the new account.

Hancock said that Dee Dee then proceeded to withdraw money from the account "very rapidly," beginning with a $250,000 cashier's check on the first day funds were available. According to him, the money was being diverted to other accounts all under Dee Dee's control.

At one point, Dee Dee even wrote a $20,000 check to Hancock himself as a token of her appreciation "for helping her keep Abraham away from the money and for helping her with future people that may be avoiding paying taxes and helping her further her rewards," the bank manager said on the stand. He told Pruner that he'd never cashed the check but instead turned it over to the bank's security office immediately. Dee Dee later asked him to return the check, claiming she had written it from the wrong account, he said.

"Sometime in March of 2009, did you receive a

phone call from Miss Moore where she appeared to be upset on the phone?" Pruner inquired.

"Yes. She called kind of frantic, possibly might be a good way to describe it, but almost hysterical. She was crying. She was concerned that some of the things that she had learned, Abraham was going to try to kill her and she didn't know what to do. She wasn't writing a book anymore, didn't want anything to do with him," Hancock explained. "It was directly involved with her handling of the money and that he was wanting to make a loan to a friend and she refused to let him, so that's what set him off and made him angry."

After that, Hancock said, Dee Dee called him repeatedly for the next several days to see if the deposit had cleared so that the funds could be accessed. He never heard from Abraham Shakespeare.

Sentorria Butler, Abraham's former girlfriend and the mother of his son Jeremiyah Kiley Shakespeare, began her testimony with her portrait of Abraham as a proud and attentive new father when their son was born, in early November 2008. Even though the couple was no longer together by that time, Abraham had attended the birth, she said, "with six cameras." And he had provided financial support for her and the new baby in the beginning.

"After we met Dee Dee, that changed," Torrie said, describing how before Dee Dee, "It was like he was excited about the birth of his son. He would come and let him lay on his chest all day long. He would just spend time there, and [then] Dee Dee came along and told

him this story and said, 'Hey, she has a lawyer. She's
going to take you for everything that you have.'"

Torrie explained that Dee Dee had convinced Abraham that the mother of his new son was after his money,
and after that, their relationship became so strained that
Abraham withheld support from her and Jeremiyah.
Judy Haggins made matters worse, Torrie said, by telling Abraham that Torrie had been having affairs with
other men and that Jeremiyah was not his child. Bereft
of support from the father of her child, Torrie did eventually file a support petition with the state, claiming
expenses of $1,950 a month for rent, utilities, food,
clothing, transportation, and child care.

It was then that Dee Dee approached the young mother
sympathetically—after having been the one whispering
innuendos in Abraham's ear.

"She was going to help me retain a lawyer and all I
had to do in return was say, yes, and of course she would
help me get a car," Torrie explained. "She offered me a
car. 'Hey, I know you like the Dodge Nitro, so I'll give
you a car if you tell me where all of the assets are so I can
tell the lawyer and we can go after Abraham.'"

The defense pounced on Sentorria Butler. Hadn't
there been more than mere arguments over the child-
support litigation and allegations of sexual infidelity?
Hileman asked. Hadn't there also been domestic abuse,
even during Ms. Butler's pregnancy? Didn't she believe
Abraham had AIDS; in fact, hadn't he told her so? And
didn't she know for a fact that Abraham had sold his
Lakeland house to Dee Dee?

As Torrie pointedly denied each allegation, Dee Dee appeared to grow more and more agitated, grimacing and sobbing. At the end of Torrie's testimony, Dee Dee shouted, "I'm tired of all these people lying. This is my life!" Her outburst seemed to infuriate the judge, who ordered a break and directed defense counsel to get their client under control.

More than once since the trial began, in fact, Judge Battles had cautioned the defense attorneys to control their client, who was more expressive in open court than the judge would abide. Dee Dee's near-constant winking, smiling, and other gestures directed at the jury was inappropriate, said the judge, and he had already found her occasional sobbing to be so disruptive that he once stopped the proceedings until the defendant regained her composure. "Miss Moore, I've cautioned you throughout these proceedings," the judge had said on the fourth day of trial. "I'm warning you. I think I'm going to make it clear for the last time."

When the trial resumed this time, the defense lawyers surprised the prosecutor and judge with an unanticipated request: they wanted to show the jurors portions of a videotaped interview Dee Dee had conducted with Torrie sometime between April and August of 2009. Hileman said he had not intended to introduce the tape, but that his client, insisting that Torrie was not telling the truth, had demanded it. The tape, explained cocounsel Christopher Boldt, would show that Ms. Butler had accused Abraham Shakespeare of domestic violence against her, that she had been told her boyfriend had AIDS, and that she was aware of the Lakeland house sale.

"Isn't it true that you actually were the victim of domestic violence?" Boldt asked Torrie soon after she returned to the stand.

"We had arguments, but not . . ." she began.

"Isn't it also true that they turned physical and you told Miss Moore on this recording that they turned physical?"

"Miss Moore approached me with a drawn-out lie of how she wanted the interview to go," Torrie said testily. "And she approached me with a story of 'Aren't you mad that Abraham left you for this girl?' and 'I'm going to show Abraham this video so that he'll come out of hiding and he'll come support this baby because if I show him this and he gets mad enough, you know, he'll come around and argue with you, Sentorria. So I want you to make this up so we can also put it in the book and then we can put it on mybabydaddy.com because I was on there with my baby . . .'"

"Okay," Boldt said, interrupting. "If I understand you correctly then, Miss Butler, it's your testimony at this point that you were not the victim of domestic violence but that you lied?"

"Yeah, she showed up with a camera and asked me to participate in her foolish thing of 'I want to make this up and put it online because I'm online with it, too.' She shows up out of the blue."

"Miss Butler, do you recall at this point saying on video that Mr. Shakespeare told you that he had AIDS?"

"His lawyer told me that he said he had it. And when she showed up with her camera to interview me, if he told his lawyer he had AIDS, then I said, 'Yeah he said he had it' because his lawyer showed up in court before a judge and under oath said, 'My client told me that he has AIDS' and I take it your lawyer just don't show up at court and lie for you."

In his redirect, Jay Pruner allowed Torrie to elaborate on Dee Dee's alleged scheme to videotape Torrie impugning Abraham with falsehoods and exaggerations in hopes of luring him out of hiding. Torrie leaped at the opportunity, giving an animated account of the plan.

"So she came and she was like, 'So I want you to go on video and I want you to go on camera and I want you to go get dressed all sexy.' Because when she came to the door, I'm looking like a gremlin. I got on a muumuu dress and kids running around. She's like, 'Go get dressed all sexy; scrunch your hair a little bit, and I'm going to get the camera and I want you to sit right here and I'm going to interview you so that we can show how nasty he is and how he doesn't do anything for his kids and just make sure that you tell them about all of the stuff he said to you last.' Like, you know, like she told me exactly what she wanted in this video."

"And you agreed and you went along with it?"

"Yes."

"All right. Thank you. Nothing further."

A large, black man strode to the witness stand, clean-shaven and neatly groomed.

Mike Smith looked far different than he had on that

January day in 2010 when he'd met with Dee Dee and Greg to discuss a $50,000 payment in exchange for confessing to the murder of Abraham Shakespeare—a ruse intended to sound like it would get Dee Dee off the hook and provide a means of support for Mike's wife and son while he was away in prison on a twenty-five-year stint.

"With whom are you employed?" asked prosecutor Jay Pruner.

"The Lake Wales Police Department," said Smith.

"How long have you been employed with the Lake Wales Police Department?"

"About thirteen years now."

"You were to be the person to accept responsibility for harming and perhaps killing Abraham Shakespeare?"

"Yes."

Like other witnesses, the undercover officer had audio recordings of his conversations with Dee Dee Moore to underscore his testimony. The astonished jurors and spectators listened as Dee Dee rattled on about her desperate situation, questioned the disposition of Smith's supposed twenty-five-year sentence, discussed how she would come up with the $50,000 to pay him to take the fall, pinned the crime on Ronald the drug dealer, and joked about Mike getting an invitation to appear on Oprah Winfrey's television show.

"Your car was wired to record the meeting?" Hileman asked the officer.

"Yes."

"How was that done, if you can explain to us just the technique you used."

"It was a remote recording device. The actual recording was taking place into the other detectives in the area." Fellow lawmen—namely, Polk County Sheriffs deputies—were listening to the whole thing as it happened, Smith explained.

Detective David Clark was recalled to the stand as the state's final witness. His testimony included even more audio recordings of Dee Dee's evasive, convoluted, and inconsistent versions of what had happened to Abraham. More dramatically, it introduced the episode in which Dee Dee blamed the shooting on her own young son.

"She said, 'My son, R. J., shot Abraham twice. Abraham was trying to choke me and R. J. walked in the room, grabbed my gun, and shot him. He was only protecting me like any son would do,'" Clark recalled. "That's what she said."

Since the beginning of the trial, journalists and courthouse observers had speculated about whether Dee Dee Moore would take the stand in her own defense. Considering the defendant's loquaciousness and seeming fondness for the limelight, many believed her testimony to be a foregone conclusion. With the state rested and the defense now ready to proceed, spectators readied themselves for what was sure to be fascinating, if likely implausible, testimony from the accused woman.

But at the start of trial, on December 10, 2012, defense

attorney Byron Hileman informed the court that although he and Christopher Boldt had spent several hours "on at least six or seven occasions" discussing the prospect of Dee Dee's testimony and had even conducted mock cross-examination to test and prepare the witness, she had ultimately decided to assert her Fifth Amendment right under the U.S. Constitution. Which meant that Dorice Donegan Moore would *not* be taking the stand.

With the defendant sworn in and standing before him, Judge Battles asked a series of questions to ensure that the decision was Dee Dee's own and not made in deference to her counsel.

"Now your decision not to testify, did you make that decision freely and voluntarily and without coercion?" Judge Battles asked.

"At the advice of my counsel and you told me to listen to my counsel," Dee Dee responded, smiling brightly and broadly.

"Well, ma'am, I want to be very, very clear here," the judge continued. "We're not going to equivocate. This is your decision. I always tell everyone that they should listen to the advice of their lawyers. That doesn't mean you necessarily follow it. This is your decision and it should be after consultation with counsel, but at the end of the day, you're making this decision, not your lawyer. Do you understand that?"

"Yes, your honor."

"All right. I'm going to ask the question again. Did you make this decision to not testify of your own free will?"

"Yes, your honor."

"Was it voluntarily?"

"Yes, your honor."

"Did anybody try to force you or bully you into that decision?"

"No, your honor."

"Did anybody try to coerce you into that decision?"

"No, your honor," Dee Dee said with a broad grin. "It just keeps my family safe."

The exchange occurred before the jury was brought in for the day's proceedings, so except for the large cache of tape recordings—and her intermittent sobbing or occasional outbursts in the courtroom—the panel would never hear from Dee Dee Moore herself.

Nor would they hear from anyone else, as it turned out. After introducing one four-page exhibit related to Dee Dee's financial dealings with Abraham's money, the defense rested without calling a single other witness to the stand. As a matter of routine, Hileman and Boldt made a motion for judgment of acquittal, a device that would have allowed the judge to usurp the jury's verdict and find Dee Dee Moore not guilty as charged.

Predictably, the motion was denied.

CHAPTER TWENTY-ONE

•••••

If jurors had lost their way through the evidence, witnesses, and exhibits presented during the two-week-long trial, assistant state's attorney James Jay Pruner was determined to get them back on track in his long, detailed closing argument.

"The reason for [Dee Dee Moore] wanting to know and meet Abraham Shakespeare is because she viewed, I suggest to you, Abraham Shakespeare much like several other people in the community had at the time—just another cash cow to milk. And milk him she did," he said, pacing before the jury box. "She was playing both ends against the middle to get one thing: her hooks into Abraham Shakespeare's last million dollars, and for added measure, she told Sentorria Butler about all of Abraham Shakespeare's sexual conquests with other women. There can be no more manipulative statement from one woman to another to drive a wedge between two people than to describe that type of contact between the parents of the same child."

Step-by- step, the assistant state's attorney revisited testimony and evidence that he said showed Dee Dee's manipulations and Abraham's gradual awareness that he'd been had and that his money was no longer under his control.

"By April thirteenth of 2009, this defendant had complete control over Abraham Shakespeare's last million dollars, had control of his house on Redhawk Bend," said Pruner. "She owned his loans on the street and what did she do? She gave several conflicting accounts of how she paid for the house." Pruner said that although Dee Dee's medical staffing company appeared to be a thriving business, greed commanded her to take advantage of the gullible Abraham Shakespeare.

"Everything, everything, everything this defendant did was about money," Pruner hammered. "That was what motivated her. That is what directed her. That is what drove her. She claims in that interview and in many statements that everything she did was because she was afraid of the drug dealers that threatened her child. It was out of fear of Ronald. But that wasn't her primary goal. And how do you know that? Because every chance she got she tried to negotiate to keep her stuff. That's what was driving her, not to keep her and her family safe."

To emphasize the point, Pruner played an excerpt from one of the many recordings with PCSO in which Dee Dee offered to tell detectives the truth if they will "cut a deal" with her, allowing her to hold onto her possessions.

"'I want a deal, I want a deal, I want a deal,'" Pruner said mockingly. "She'll give the person's name. Not 'Keep me safe, keep me out of harm's way,' but 'You let me keep my stuff, I'll roll, I'll tell you the person's name.' I want a deal; that was her motivation."

Despite spending considerable time and energy establishing a possible motive for premeditated murder, Pruner reminded the jury that the state was not even required to prove motive.

Nonetheless, he urged the jury to consider the "why."

"And the why is because she got every bit of his money," Pruner thundered. "Abraham Shakespeare found out about it, threatened to kill her, and she killed him first. And everything that she did after that was with the same goal in mind as she had up front—to get and to preserve her, what she considered her money. As soon as this defendant killed Abraham Shakespeare, she began an elaborate, detailed, multi-front campaign to conceal his whereabouts and his death."

Defense counsel Byron Hileman began his closing argument with a distinguishing characteristic of the case: he noted that Dee Dee Moore had not been charged with financial misbehaviors like fraud or embezzlement. She was charged with first-degree, premeditated murder. Furthermore, Hileman said, given that the state's case was predominantly circumstantial—a characterization that the state readily acknowledged—he insisted that the jurors should consider a reasonable hypothesis of innocence. In other words, the possibility that Abraham Shakespeare had ended up shot and buried on Dee Dee Moore's property without her having been the person who killed or buried him.

"If you listen to the tapes, we believe the evidence will show you if you consider them as a totality, that this is a desperate, panicked, perhaps emotionally unstable woman finding herself in an impossible situation trying to find an explanation that can salvage her life and her son's life," Hileman offered. "That is an alternative explanation of those facts that you must weigh and you must ask yourself if the state has presented sufficient evidence to exclude that possible interpretation of the evidence because if it has not in your opinion, then that constitutes reasonable doubt."

By the end of her attorney's closing argument, Dee Dee Moore was a red-faced, tear-soaked mess, her sobs, grunts, and moans causing a scene. Judge Battles sent the jurors out of the courtroom for a fifteen-minute "comfort break."

While the jurors were out, the judge said to the defense attorneys, "I want you to talk to her again," pointing to Dee Dee.

"You are to compose yourself," he continued, glaring at the defendant. "That is to stop, do you understand me?"

"Yes, sir," Dee Dee sniffled as the judge left the bench in a huff.

Many high-profile cases are bedeviled by wrangling over jury instructions, that all-important blueprint for deliberations. By the time attorneys for the state and attorneys for the defense reached that stage with the judge, there was only one bone of contention between the two sides. But it was a big one. The state had acknowledged that its case against Dee Dee Moore was largely circumstantial—no eyewitnesses, no confession, and no hard evidence that Dee Dee killed Abraham Shakespeare. Now, the defense wanted to make sure the jury understood that the state not only had no concrete evidence that Dee Dee had committed a murder, but, more important, had no hard proof that it involved premeditation—the part that drove the charge to a capital offense. Hileman wanted the jurors to get the "classic" instruction about circumstantial evidence, which strenuously discouraged conviction on circumstantial evidence. But that instruction had been usurped two decades earlier, when the Florida Supreme Court decided the instruction might lead jurors to believe that circumstantial evidence was inferior to hard evidence, leaving them confused and possibly tempted to dismiss it altogether. So, the state's highest court made the classic instruction an option for judges and here was Hileman urging Judge Battles to exercise it. Pruner, champing for conviction, argued against that. Judge Battles respectfully denied Hileman's request to include the old instruction.

Reconvened in the jury box, the men and women who would decide Dee Dee Moore's fate sat quietly and attentively as the judge began reading the lengthy instructions.

"To prove the crime of first-degree premeditated murder, the state must prove the following three elements beyond a reasonable doubt," he said. "One, Abraham Shakespeare is dead. Two, the death was caused by the criminal act of Dorice Donegan Moore. Three, there was a premeditated killing of Abraham Shakespeare." He then explained that, under the law, premeditated murder required a conscious decision to kill, regardless of how much or little time passed between the decision to kill and the homicidal act.

"It will be sufficient proof of premeditation if the circumstances of the killing and the conduct of the accused convince you beyond a reasonable doubt of the existence of premeditation at the time of the killing," said Judge Battles.

The jurors' options to convict on a lesser crime were spelled out next. The panel could find Dee Dee guilty of second-degree murder if they believed she killed Abraham by "an act imminently dangerous to another and demonstrating a depraved mind without regard for human life." They could choose manslaughter if they believed Dee Dee "intentionally committed an act or acts that caused the death of Abraham Shakespeare," provided it was not by negligence or a justifiable homicide. They would also have to decide whether Dee Dee Moore discharged a firearm to commit the crime.

"Now, the constitution requires the state to prove its accusation against the defendant," the judge informed the jury. "It is not necessary for the defendant to disprove anything, nor is a defendant required to prove her innocence. It is up to the state to prove the defendant's guilt by evidence. The defendant exercised a fundamental right by choosing not to be a witness in this case." He cautioned the jurors against drawing any conclusions about

Dee Dee's guilt or innocence based on her decision not to take the stand.

Between November 2009, when Abraham Shakespeare was officially reported missing, and January 29, 2010, when the human remains retrieved from Dee Dee Moore's backyard were positively identified as Abraham's, Dee Dee had offered investigators a litany of scenarios—first about the man's disappearance and then his death and burial. Through tapes and testimony, the jury had heard them all.

But the state had only one theory for the jury to consider: Dee Dee Moore had found an easy target to satisfy her greed—an unsophisticated man with millions at his disposal. She had tricked him into turning over control of his money to her, primarily by leading him to believe that the mother of his young son was out to take his fortune away and that transferring his assets to Dee Dee would keep the money out of the ex-girlfriend's hands. But then, the state posited, Abraham became rightly suspicious that Dee Dee was spending his money on herself, and he confronted her in her office at 5732 State Road 60 in April 2009. An argument ensued. When Abraham presumably threatened Dee Dee, either with bodily harm or with turning her in, Dee Dee then pulled out her gun and shot him twice in the chest. She planned to bury his body in her backyard and called her ex-husband, James (who was in the excavation business), to dig a hole, ostensibly to bury some trash. But James was concerned that the equipment would hit underground power and water lines, so Dee Dee directed him to dig the trash hole next door, in the backyard of the house she also owned, at 5802 State Road 60. He did that and left, returning just before dark to fill in the hole, by then filled with debris. A few days later, the concrete contractor who had poured Dee Dee's driveway at the 5802 house returned to pour a thirty-by-thirty-foot concrete slab in the backyard, from where Abraham Shakespeare's murdered body was exhumed on January 28, 2010.

The defense, which had presented no witnesses nor a single piece of evidence related to Dee Dee's financial dealings, asked the jurors to indulge their doubts about the state's theory. Wasn't it possible that there really *were* bad guys afoot—drug dealers who had shot and killed Abraham and who'd forced Dee Dee to help them cover it up or else be killed or watch her young son be killed? Might not these fiends have killed Abraham and buried him on Dee Dee's property to blackmail her into cooperating with them? And had not Greg Smith, the confidential informant, helped lead Dee Dee down the road of evasion and cover-up by suggesting certain actions to mislead investigators? All of these were reasonable possibilities that deserved the jury's serious consideration, the defense counsel argued, and any doubt they engendered should be enough to acquit their client.

As the deliberations began, so did the guessing game about which way the jury would go.

As usual, observers had tried to read the jurors throughout the trial, noting every frown or scowl, every smile, yawn, shifting of seats, and taking of notes to mean something. But what? There was a lot of speculation too about

Dee Dee's antics during the proceedings and whether her sobbing and outbursts had made the jurors feel some sympathy for the woman, who insisted she had only tried to help a man whose riches had left him poor in spirit.

Only the twelve men and women in the jury room could provide the answers, and since they had been prohibited from discussing the case even with one another to that point, they would have to figure out where they stood by themselves.

The commencement of jury deliberations on the afternoon of December 10, 2012, meant that witnesses could finally leave the holding room and move around without restriction, speaking and mingling as they wished. Spectators too, earlier prohibited from talking or gesturing during the trial, were now free to talk and could go and come as they pleased. The attorneys were in recess as well, although the judge asked them not to go farther than fifteen minutes away in case the jurors had a question. The two alternates on the jury were released, free to leave the courthouse or, if they preferred, to stay and wait out the verdict with the rest of the courtroom.

With the jurors safely ensconced in a guarded room, some of the tensions that had gripped the courtroom during the prior two weeks eased. Throughout the trial, the attorneys and judge had been so edgy about protecting the appearance of fairness that, a few times, their precautions bordered on the laughable. The first instance came just days into the proceedings when a female juror told the bailiff, who then told the judge, that she had been sitting outside reading a book during the lunch recess when a spectator came up to her and said, "It must be hard to be a juror." The woman said she replied, "I can't talk about that," and there was no further interaction. Still, the juror reported the encounter, mindful of the judge's standard admonition to jurors not to discuss the case among themselves, with anyone else, or even allow anyone to discuss it in their presence. "Remember," he'd told them, "if anyone attempts to say anything to you or in your presence, that's when you tell them you're on the jury trying this case. You tell them to immediately stop. If that person persists, you leave them. The very next opportunity, as soon as possible, you tell a bailiff, who in turn will advise me."

"Judge, I also would like to make a revelation," defense attorney Byron Hileman said after the juror's brief interaction was mentioned. "I can't remember his name, but the elderly gentleman on the jury, he and I ran into each other in the doorway of the bathroom. And we almost ran into each other, and I said, 'Hi.'"

Hileman was not being sarcastic or snippy. Normally, such a minor encounter would not warrant a mention. But Hileman was antsy about any little thing that might be construed as improper. Everyone was.

"I'm going to make absolutely clear to everyone assembled, to all counsel, so they can also make it clear to anyone else attending that they're associated with, there is going to be absolutely, strictly no contact with any of these jurors as we go about this proceeding," Judge Battles declared, putting both brief encounters to rest. "That's how we ensure a fair trial. And I want to make that clear to everyone."

A few days later, a transcriber for In Session, the company broadcasting the trial, reported to the court another interaction with the same older male juror, who turned out to be the foreman, Roger Gaines.

"Around 12:30 I was on the way back to this annex with my lunch. One of the jurors said, 'Can I ask you a question?' Immediately I recognized that he was a juror and I said, 'I'm sorry, I can't talk to you. You are a juror.' And he said, 'I just want to ask you a question. What are you doing over there? Are you transcribing?' So my response to him was, 'More or less,' and I kept walking."

It was enough to get Gaines called before the judge, who told the juror that although he understood Gaines's question was probably innocent, it still violated the court's rules.

"I'll remind you, and hopefully in a most tactful way, that that admonishment I give about not talking with anyone about the case or anything to do with the case, including their technical role and all, is a very broad one," the judge said.

"I didn't think that I was talking about the case," Gaines said sheepishly.

"I understand."

"I had no intention of doing that."

"I understand that, sir. And I certainly understand that. Do you believe any of this, including my inquiry or anything, affects in any way your ability to be fair and impartial in this matter?"

"No, not at all."

On a couple of occasions, however, the judge got wind of more serious concerns from the jurors. Early in the trial, several members of the panel reported feeling intimidated by Abraham's friends and family, individuals whom the jurors felt had been glaring at them both during the trial and during breaks. Although none of the jurors could cite any specific threat, Judge Battles assigned guards to accompany the members during their comings and goings at the courthouse. Another curious incident occurred in the courtroom at the very end of the trial, as lawyers for both sides were wrapping up their cases. With no context or details provided, Judge Battles asked a stockily built woman with eyebrow piercings and short, slicked-back hair to stand.

"It's been reported to the court that you may have engaged in conversations which may be construed as threats to witnesses in this case," the judge said to her. "Accordingly, you are now being excluded from these proceedings. You will go outside where law enforcement will have an opportunity, as appropriate, to interview you. Now, step out."

Outside the courtroom, the woman identified herself as Rose Condora, a friend of Dee Dee's. They had been in Tampa's Orient Road Jail together, she told reporters, and since her release, she had visited Dee Dee every night.

"On one of my visits, she had told me that one of the witnesses chased down one of the jurors on her way to her car," Rose explained. "And I said something needed to chase him down to kick his ass, in plain English. So apparently that's a threat and the judge excluded me now from his courtroom."

Nothing more ever came of the incident, but it was an example of how seriously the court took its charge to keep the trial—and the jury—safe from outside influences and stress. And another example of how skilled Dee Dee was at manipulating people into feeling defensive and protective of her.

It was early evening on December 10, 2012, after-hours at the Hillsborough County Courthouse in Tampa, but the lights still shone brightly. Courthouse employees who normally would have headed home after a day's work lingered with the crowd around Judge Battles's courtroom. Townspeople on their way home stopped by in hopes of witnessing the finale of a case that had captured the public fascination for years. Abraham's family and friends huddled anxiously, hopeful that the difficult life of their loved one would at least end with a bit of justice.

A little more than three hours after deliberations began, word came that the jurors had reached a verdict. Spectators and attorneys nervously returned to the courtroom, abuzz with speculation about what the jury's relatively quick decision meant. Some predicted the defendant would walk free because the jurors had not been given enough hard evidence to convict. Others were just as sure the swift return was bad news for Dee Dee, a sign that the state had made a slam dunk as far as the jury was concerned. Either way, it was clear the jury had not suffered any major qualms. That's what short deliberations meant: one side or the other had proved its case decisively in the jurors' eyes.

"*State of Florida versus Dorice Donegan Moore*, Case 10-CF-1733," the clerk began as a hush fell over the courtroom and Dee Dee and her attorneys stood at attention.

The jury foreman spoke. "We, the jury find as follows as to Count 1 of the charge: the defendant is guilty of first-degree murder. The defendant did actually possess and discharge a firearm causing death. So say we all, dated this tenth day of December, Robert Gaines, foreperson of the jury."

Dressed in a black dress and a heather-gray blazer, Dee Dee shook her head slowly as the jurors were polled individually, each affirming the verdict. Spectators shifted in their seats, clasped their hands over their mouths. Several mimed, "Oh my God." Abraham's sister wept. Other relatives embraced Elizabeth Walker. The courtroom was now a quiet but animated theater of raw emotion.

The jury's work complete, Judge Battles thanked them for their service and dismissed them, freeing them to resume their ordinary lives and freeing them also to speak—or not—about the case as much as they wanted.

"For centuries, our society has relied upon juries just like you for consideration of difficult cases, and we've recognized for hundreds of years that your deliberations, your discussions, your votes should remain your private affair as long as you wish it. So the law gives you the unique privilege not to speak about the jury's work. Now, there is another side of that coin. Just as you are at liberty to refuse to speak to anyone, you are now at liberty to speak to anyone about your deliberations."

No sooner had the jury left the room than Judge Battles prepared to pronounce sentence. The state had said years before that it would not seek the death penalty; Dee Dee Moore could thank Elizabeth Walker for that. According to Christopher Lynn, the Polk County homicide detective who worked so closely with Wallace and Clark on the case and now a sergeant in the sheriff's office, it was Abraham Shakespeare's mother who spared Dee Dee's life. Although the state has the prerogative to ask for the ultimate penalty in capital-murder cases, some state's attorneys make a habit of conferring with the victim's family in case they have religious, moral, or other qualms that would make the death penalty unacceptable to them.

"Had it not been for the graciousness of Elizabeth Walker, Dee Dee Moore would be facing the needle now," said Lynn. "This seventy-five-year-old Christian lady—I don't even know if she would swat a fly but she knows that this woman killed her son, treated him like a piece of trash, and she says, 'No, [Dee Dee] can live.'"

With the death penalty removed as an option, life in prison without the possibility of parole was foregone under the state's sentencing guidelines. The judge invited comments from both sides, including victim-impact statements from Abraham's family, but no one stepped forth, so Judge Battles turned directly to the defendant, who stood facing him.

"Miss Moore," the judge said somberly, "after listening to all of this over two weeks, words that were said here—

cold, *calculated*, *cruel*—they all apply. *Manipulative*. Probably the most manipulative person that this court has seen. Abraham Shakespeare was your prey and your victim. Money was the root of the evil that you brought to Abraham, and now I'm going to pronounce the sentence."

Although she had repeatedly cried, sometimes uncontrollably, throughout the trial, Dee Dee was a portrait of composure as the judge condemned her.

"For the murder of Abraham Shakespeare, you are sentenced to life imprisonment, and you shall not be eligible for parole. To the extent chapter 775.0087 requires it, I will also pronounce a twenty-five-year minimum mandatory pursuant to that statute. The sentence of life without parole is also mandatory."

To which, Dee Dee nodded as calmly as she would if being advised on where to park her car. It was yet another oddity in the saga of Dee Dee Moore. She had collapsed into hysterics so many times throughout the trial that even the judge had stormed out once. Yet here she was, being sentenced to spend the rest of her days behind bars, taking the news sedately.

Within minutes, Dorice Donegan Moore was fingerprinted, handcuffed, and led away by deputies to begin serving the rest of her life in the custody of the Florida State prison system. That evening, some of Abraham's friends celebrated at a Tampa hotel, toasting Greg Smith as the hero of the case, the man who had delivered the two-sided coin of justice to Dee Dee Moore and to Abraham Shakespeare. The man who had outwitted a shameless and murdering con artist.

CHAPTER TWENTY-TWO

▪▪▪▪▪

At least a couple of jurors wasted no time taking advantage of their newfound license to discuss the case that had consumed two weeks of their lives. A day after rendering the verdict, Roger Gaines, the jury foreman, talked with Tampa television station WTSP, telling the reporter that during the trial, the case had kept him up at night as the proceedings replayed in his head, raising more questions.

Both Roger Gaines and Arthur Williams, another retiree on the jury who spoke to the press after the trial, said that the proximity of the two bullet wounds in Abraham Shakespeare's chest had been the single most compelling piece of evidence in their decision to convict. The shots wouldn't have happened that way if, as Dee Dee had maintained, the shooting had been the result of a struggle.

"Bam, bam!" Arthur Williams said. "As one juror demonstrated, the bullet holes would only be side by side if someone wanted to put them there on purpose. If the gun is waving around, it wouldn't be side by side. But she shot the first bullet, then the second one."

Ironically, Dee Dee's videotaped interview with Abraham shortly before his disappearance—a tape she had counted on to accredit her claim that Abraham had gone into hiding—only served to convince the jurors that the defendant had been thinking ahead about how to cover up the deadly deed that would follow. And all the sobbing, gesturing, and outbursts that Dee Dee might have hoped would engender sympathy for her? "Theatrics," Roger Gaines told the news station.

According to him, the deliberations began with nine jurors voting for first-degree murder and three leaning toward second-degree murder. Calm, respectful discussions eventually persuaded the three to make the first-degree verdict unanimous. The foreman called the state's case "airtight."

"She thought she could talk her way out of anything," he said. "In some ways, she is smart. She set up LLCs, laundered money. But, in other ways, she wasn't smart. She was a manipulator."

Neither man had much to say about the defense case, such as it was. "I don't know what they could have done," Roger Gaines said, shaking his head. "How could they put on a case? Maybe call a few character witnesses? The prosecution did a great job. The defense just didn't have a case."

* * *

Never let it be said that Dee Dee Moore did not put up a valiant effort to hold onto the bounty she had purloined from Abraham Shakespeare. Just because she was never able to "cut a deal" with law enforcement—and even though her former boyfriend had already surrendered the Corvette she had given him as a Valentine's Day gift—did not mean she was done trying to keep the house, the jewelry, and various other goods she had amassed at Abraham's expense.

A year before her murder trial, Dee Dee had taken the stand in a Hillsborough County Circuit Court hearing on her motion to reclaim the jewelry, expensive handbags, financial documents, and other personal property that had been seized in connection with the murder trial. She cried on the stand, telling the judge that she "didn't steal a dime" and insisting that all the items, including those turned over by her own mother nearly two years earlier, were rightfully hers. Although her lawyer argued that many of the items had been purchased before Dee Dee even met Abraham Shakespeare and offered to make copies of the financial documents for prosecutors while taking custody of the originals, Judge Ronald Ficarrotta denied the request, ruling that the documents were relevant to the criminal case and the personal property was part of a civil lawsuit filed by Abraham Shakespeare's estate.

Dee Dee lost again in October 2013, when another court ordered the Lakeland house on Redhawk Bend

Drive—the house Abraham had bought for himself but that Dee Dee had moved into in early 2009—returned to Abraham's family. The judge found that despite Dee Dee's claims to have purchased the house from Abraham, there was no proof that she'd ever paid him. Circuit Judge J. Dale Durrance also ordered that some of the mortgage loan accounts that Dee Dee had taken over from Abraham—ostensibly to unburden him—be returned to the deceased man's estate.

Earlier, the Shakespeare family's lawyer, Stephen Martin, had succeeded in getting other property turned over to the estate, including a Silverado pickup truck owned by Dee Dee and the house at 5802 State Road 60, where Abraham's remains were found. The house had been stripped of its appliances and electronic equipment before ownership was transferred, but Martin said the properties would be sold to provide much-needed funds for supporting Abraham's two sons, Moses and Jeremiyah.

The estate also sued the Bank of America, charging negligence and breach of fiduciary duty to Abraham in setting up the account from which his name was removed as signatory and that Dee Dee had immediately plundered.

The complaint, filed in April 2013 by an attorney appointed by the probate court to represent Shakespeare's estate, listed thirteen violations, including "negligently dealing with allowing Dorice 'Dee Dee' Moore to set up an account to commit and be used for criminal acts and allowing the wrongful acts to be perpetrated without properly considering, investigating, or heeding all the suspicious facts and circumstances that should have raised concern and questions to any reasonable person." The suit also said the bank neglected "to report evidence of exploitation [that] Defendant knew or reasonably should have known or had cause to suspect."

The filing included a copy of the poorly constructed document Dee Dee had submitted as purported proof that Abraham Shakespeare, LLC had authorized the bank to remove Abraham's signing rights. Dee Dee had provided nothing but a plain white sheet of paper, with no letterhead, address, or even the name of the LLC, with a heading that read "Minutes Meeting" and dated February 17, 2009. Under "Present," it read simply, "Dee Dee Moore." Under "Agenda," it said, "Remove Abraham Shakespeare from the business account."

The document listed no other agenda items and directed the recipient to call Dee Dee Moore "with additions or corrections to these minutes." It ended with her own signature.

The lawsuit noted that Dee Dee had emptied the account of more than a million dollars in a mere five days, making two $250,000 withdrawals on February 18, 2009; $200,000 on February 19; and another $250,000 on February 23. It said the $20,000 check to Doug Hancock was delivered to the bank's security department, "and it was placed in a safe deposit box to which he had no access." One of the first withdrawals was by cashier's check made payable to the Internal Revenue Service. The endorsement on the back of the check said "not used for purpose intended." The cashier's check was then deposited into an account belonging to American Medical Professionals, LLC, Dee Dee's medical staffing company.

Regional counsel Byron Hileman seemed resigned to the outcome and at peace with himself. "I can sleep good at night because I know I had done the very best job," he told reporters. "I feel sad for the victim. I feel sad for their families. I feel sad for the defendant because these types of cases are no-win situations."

The burly defense attorney would have two more pieces of business with Dee Dee Moore before he was done with the sensational case. In January 2013, he asked the court to order a new trial, arguing that his client had been convicted solely on circumstantial evidence—the premise of his closing argument during trial. "The evidence at trial we believe simply did not meet the legal standards of sufficiency in that the state did not adduce evidence of substantial, competent evidence to exclude any hypothesis of innocence regarding the issue of premeditation," he argued. Judge Battles politely denied the motion.

At that same hearing, Judge Battles also signed an order declaring Dee Dee Moore to be indigent and appointing a state-sponsored attorney in a different circuit to handle her case henceforth. In January 2013, Hileman filed a notice of appeal with the Thirteenth Judicial Circuit of Florida, challenging how the trial court handled a November 2012 pretrial hearing in which Dee Dee was found competent to stand trial, the court's denial of the defense motion to suppress Dee Dee's interview with detectives after Abraham's remains were recovered—sessions in which she admitted to having poured lime over the dead man's remains; the sentencing process; the denial of Hileman's motion for a new trial; and the entire jury trial as judicial acts the bases for appeal. For a case with such a high-profile and serious felony, an appeal was fully expected.

Elizabeth Walker removed the framed scroll that she'd once displayed in a window of her modest home. "Bless this home, oh Lord we pray. Fill it with your love today. May friends and family so dear, know your peace as they enter here," it read. She had found the words comforting and encouraging but could no longer abide the memento itself, considering that it had been a gift from Dee Dee Moore. Speaking with a Tampa Bay television reporter, Elizabeth lamented Abraham's last years of life, proclaiming him a "good-hearted" son whom she wished she could thank for "who he was." And as for her son's killer: "I already have forgiven her. Yes, I have. I have to forgive her, because that's what the Master says."

EPILOGUE

■ ■ ■ ■ ■

Only four cities in the United States can legitimately claim to be a "horse capital of the world," and Ocala, Florida, is one of them. Carl G. Rose saw to that back in 1943, when he discovered that the area's soil was rich in limestone, not unlike the legendary Kentucky bluegrasses, so he purchased a bunch of acres along a state highway and carved out a Thoroughbred horse farm among the oaks that he named Rosemere Farm. The area soon sprouted other horse farms, including Harbor View Farm, whose chestnut stallion, Affirmed, won the coveted Triple Crown in 1978 and helped cinch Marion County and its county seat, Ocala, as a major hub of Thoroughbred farms. There are more than 1,200 such farms in Marion County today and another 300 that raise other top-quality equines.

The pastoral landscapes, along with abundant sunshine

and warm temperatures, have also made Ocala a choice destination for retirees. The county is dotted with retirement communities, including one so serious about maintaining peace and quiet for its aging residents that no one under the age of nineteen is allowed to live there.

Ocala is also home to the Lowell Correctional Institute, one of the women's units in the Florida Department of Corrections system. In 2001, Lowell opened TRF Farm with forty-two retired Florida-bred Thoroughbred horses; fifteen inmates are allowed to work at the farm for a year, grooming the animals and tending to their stables. Most depart with a certificate in equine-grooming technology—something they can put to use when they are released from prison.

Though not by her choosing, Ocala is also where Dee Dee Moore will live out the rest of her days. As Florida inmate number T30310, the woman who once lived in a luxurious home in a gated community now claims a bed in a dormitory she shares with up to eighty female prisoners. And even if self-esteem and a sense of purpose were challenges for Dee Dee Moore, she would not be allowed to participate in Lowell's acclaimed horse-farm program because she has no release date. Her job at the institution is that of dorm worker, helping clean and maintain the large, communal living space for a variety of female offenders. Most days, she is allowed to spend some time in the prison's enclosed outdoor yard, with its shady pavilion and sun-drenched benches. Every Saturday, Sunday, and state-recognized holiday, she is allowed to have a visitor or two.

When she's not working in the dorm, T30310 may watch television in the annex's day room. Or she may listen to music on a radio or digital player purchased from the prison canteen. She has borrower's privileges at the prison library and may also check out books from the prison chapel. The annex has five levels of custody: maximum, close, medium, minimum, and community. Dee Dee is under "close" custody, meaning her movements are constantly monitored, sometimes recorded, and invariably restricted. Prison officials say there have been no disciplinary actions against Dee Dee since she began serving time.

Now confined, her worldly possessions reduced to a few toiletries, cosmetics, CDs, and books, about the only thing Dee Dee Moore has been able to hold onto since her conviction has been her adamant denial of guilt and her insistence that she only participated in covering up Abraham Shakespeare's murder in order to protect her and her son's lives. In an exclusive interview, Matt Gutman, a correspondent for the venerable ABC news show *20/20*, sat with the convicted murderer in the cafeteria of her cell block at Lowell. The segment, which aired on *20/20* in September 2013, was titled "Crazy, Stupid Luck."

Dee Dee Moore was shown entering the cafeteria wearing bluish-gray prison-issue shirt and pants, smiling broadly, and carrying a stack of loose-leaf papers. The guard who escorted her to the room could be heard offering reassurances that the interview would go smoothly, but Dee Dee did not take the encouragement graciously.

"I'm not nervous," she said dismissively. "I don't get nervous."

Gutman plunged right in.

"Did you murder Abraham Shakespeare?" he asked.

"Absolutely not," Dee Dee said, grinning.

"Did you bury him in your backyard?"

"Absolutely not," she said again, now on the verge of giggling.

Gutman made note of Dee Dee's broad smile and lightheartedness, both unseemly given the grim subject matter. Why was she was laughing when a man had been murdered? Gutman asked. Still grinning, Dee Dee said that it was because she found the accusations against her—accusations that a jury had duly considered and affirmed by convicting her—to be "entertaining."

She told the network correspondent that she had known Abraham Shakespeare for only four months, and it was absurd to think she would meet him and plot his murder in so short a spell. Besides, she said, she had fans in high places—movie producers who want to put the sordid tale on the big screen.

Rather than indulge Dee Dee's braggadocio, Gutman asked her to explain how she came to be involved with Abraham in the first place, a story he had already researched but needed to hear from the horse's mouth.

She would tell the newsman what she had told detectives, Abraham's friends and family, and anyone else who asked—that she was simply a kindhearted person who saw someone in need of help and "jumped in." On that part of the story, Dee Dee had always been consistent.

Then how did things get so out of hand? Gutman asked.

Dee Dee blamed it on a lack of street smarts, suggesting that naïveté left her susceptible to unsavory characters who might entangle her—unwittingly, of course—in their immoral and illegal schemes. As Dee Dee switched from confident, even cocky, to sorrowful and reflective, Gutman took advantage of the mood change. He asked her how she felt about the jury's verdict, and the question provoked a fit of tears.

"They murdered me by the hands of justice; I'm murdered," she sobbed, with no apparent sense of the irony in decrying the same crime for which she had been convicted. "You might as well kill me 'cause this is no type of living in here. I would never harm another human being. I would never hurt nobody. I liked Mickey Mouse and Donald Duck and Disney. I liked Tinkerbell and kids. I'm not a mean person. I know I'll go to heaven; God knows I'm innocent. That's one person that knows I'm innocent."

Gutman stared at Dee Dee in amazement as she wallowed in denial, self-pity, and finger-pointing while volunteering that she couldn't blame the jurors for their verdict because the defense had presented no case of its own. "They didn't get to hear my side," she said, claiming her absence from the witness stand was at her lawyers' urging, not by her own preference. Even though she had calmly told Judge Battles several times that the decision not to testify was her own—that she chose to refrain from testifying to protect her family—she now said that her lawyers, Byron Hileman and Christopher Boldt, told her she didn't need to take the stand. In the *20/20* piece,

Gutman reported that Hileman denied Dee Dee's claim and insisted that it was Dee Dee's decision not to testify.

Regarding her claim that she had been framed for Abraham's murder, Dee Dee said she was set up because she was an easy target whom the perpetrators manipulated by threatening to kill her son. Investigators had consistently ignored that possibility, she said angrily. They had also ignored DNA evidence at the crime scene that would have led them to the real murderers, she maintained. As Gutman knew, investigators had never reported any evidence of mysterious third parties, drug dealers, or otherwise. Nor had they found any suspicious DNA at the crime scene.

When Gutman inquired if she had ever sexually propositioned one of the detectives on the case, as Dave Clark had testified, she stopped her whimpering and became, once again, self-assured.

"Absolutely," she said, explaining that the mythical Ronald had told her that Detective Clark was pretending to sympathize with her and that she should flirt with him. She did not explain what purpose that flirtation was to serve other than perhaps to alert her as to when detectives were recording their conversations with her since, according to Ronald, "He's not recording you when he's flirting with you." Dee Dee told Gutman that she went along with it because her life was at stake.

"Do you understand how listening to you is bewildering?" Gutman asked, the incredulity plain on his face.

"Well, do you understand how listening to you is

just, it sounds like a bunch of stupidity?" she shot back. Gutman, she said, was just another pawn of the legal system.

"You're trying to convict me," she charged, as if no verdict had already been pronounced.

Obviously irritated by Gutman's challenges, Dee Dee shuffled through the papers she had brought with her to the interview. They contained witness statements, she said. Witnesses who knew what really happened. Witnesses who could exonerate her. Witnesses investigators had ignored.

Dee Dee waved the stack of papers at Gutman. But when he reached for them and told her the network would be happy to contact the untapped witnesses for their purportedly exculpatory accounts, she yanked the papers back out of reach, explaining that she would have to get the witnesses' permission first because the case was ongoing. Then she plucked a single page from the stack and flashed it at one of the network cameras.

"This is stuff that's not in my discovery," she said. "These are witness statements."

Gutman was having none of it. He told Dee Dee that there were no such witnesses and that, from what he could see, the scribblings on the pages looked like her handwriting.

For a moment, Dee Dee was speechless and seemed disoriented. "Wh-what do you mean?" she stammered.

"Why don't you give [us] the witnesses and we'll investigate," Gutman said. "You want me to get the story straight; I'm happy to investigate it."

Dee Dee scoffed at Gutman's offer to get to the bottom of her claims, dramatically gathering her papers and heading toward the exit in a huff. Gutman continued to press for a name—any name—of a witness who could corroborate Dee Dee's story and attest to Ronald's existence, if not his involvement in Abraham's death.

"Her first name is Deanna, I'll give you that," she said, before disappearing behind the heavy doors.

The outrageousness of Dee Dee's parting shot was not lost on detectives. The only time they had heard the name "Deanna" was from Angelina Marshall, who had been in Tampa's Orient Jail the same time Dee Dee was there awaiting transfer to prison. Three years prior, Angelina had told a Hillsborough County detective of a cellmate named Deanna who had overheard Dee Dee enlisting Angelina to help recover hidden caches of money, jewelry, and other belongings so that the courts could not confiscate them. Now, out of nowhere, Dee Dee was throwing Deanna's name out as investigative bait.

"Typical Dee Dee Moore," said David Clark, now a sergeant with the Polk County Sheriff's Office. "She'll go down in her grave trying to blame this on somebody else. People have asked me if I think she will ever come clean and I say, absolutely not. Dee Dee will die in prison still claiming her innocence."

AFTERWORD

In early January 2013, defense attorneys Byron Hileman and Christopher Boldt, whose services to Dee Dee Moore are paid by Florida's taxpayers, notified the Hillsborough Circuit Court that they were going to appeal Dee Dee's murder conviction. Later that month, they filed the requisite documents in Florida's Second District Court of Appeals in Lakeland. At the time this book was published, appellate procedures were still underway and the court had not yet scheduled a hearing of the case.